WORKING IT:

DISRUPTION RULES

2020 EDITION

Making the future work:

We are standing at the dawn of a new era.

Infinite possibilities.

Amazing opportunities.

Where our hopes and dreams can be realized.

And our passions will guide us.

And our Humanity and joys will fulfill us.

If only we could get out of our own way and stop shooting ourselves in the foot.

Making the Future Work 2015 - 2020, Search for a Simpler Way Study

FREE STUFF
AND, THERE'S MORE …

I was taught about work from the company's indoctrination and onboarding program and 300-page employee compliance manuals. It was almost like understanding my work from a distance. I was an engineer and was expected to engineer whatever that meant.

Today, things are different. Work today is confusing and messy. There is little training with lots of misunderstood expectations. The more context and points of view you have, the better you'll be equipped for change. I want you, the reader, see yourself as an active participant, owner, and navigator in the game of your work.

So, we have a few resources for you. Visit **WorkingIt.com** for 100's of work articles.

Visit **Insights.CERMAcademy.com** for 1000's of **FREE** VUCA, risk articles, courses, etc.

Visit **AsianChixWithAttitude.com** for **Working It** merch & attitude.

Experts are Standing By:

Victoria Lai for keynotes on Asian work styles, retailpocalypse, and the *Future of Work* in Asia at Victoria@WorkingIt.com or 503.317.8892.

Margaux Hutchins for keynotes on the *Future of Work*; Working with Gen-Z'ers; Surviving College, etc. at Margaux@WorkingIt.com or 503.757.6513.

Greg Hutchins PE CERM for information on the *Future of Work* at 503.233.1012 or GregH@europa.com.

© 2019 by Gregory Hutchins PE CERM

Finally, I dedicate this book to the millions of people (Vucans) who wonder what's going on at work, what they can do about it, and how to get a job. As well, dozens of people patiently reviewed **Working It: Disruption Rules - 2020 Edition**. None walked away unscathed. Many liked it. Others had very strong feelings and comments on the future of jobs, work, and careers. Thank you all.

TABLE OF CONTENTS

CONTEXT

—

WORTH 20 IQ POINTS

WHAT'S WORKING IT?

T-Mobile For Business Ad in the *Wall Street Journal* distills the essence of **Working It: Disruption Rules**:

"Business is Changing. Are You With Us?"

"Business is changing. Upstarting. Restarting. Jumpstarting. 30,000 feet working. Texting. Pinging. Posting. Next-day delivering. Thinking. Rethinking. Buying. Selling. Flexible-hours demanding. Sharing. Blogging. Open-floor plan rethinking. Designing. Differentiating. Co-working. Downloading. Uploading. Video-conference calling. Digitizing. Automating. Work-life balancing. Mobilizing. Streaming. Outsourcing. Cross-country-cloud collaborating. Animating. Coding. Diversifying. Deep diving. Innovating. Disrupting."[1]

WHAT'S THE SOLUTION?

"Whether you work in industry, the nonprofit sector or government, there is no way to anticipate and plan for the new structure and operational rules that are unfolding. ... The only way to successfully navigate the level of change is to be a fluid and creative problem solver. That's why the World Economic Forum labeled complex problem-solving the number one skill for the twenty-first century. Organizations everywhere are looking for this capability in their talent recruiting above all else."[2]

CONTEXT Drivers

Old School	New School
Gutenbergs	Digital natives
Cost, quality, schedule work filters	Risk work filter
Static work rules	Dynamic work rules, boundary conditions, tools, and expectations
Evolutionary change	Disruptive change
Evolutionary tech	Disruptive tech
Lifelong employment	Just-in-time & value-added employment (gig-work)
Life lesson learned	Work Lesson Earned
Moore's employment half-life 10 or more years	Moore's employment half-life 3 or fewer years
Transactional work	Process and systems work frameworks
Focus on past & today	Focus on the *Future of Work*
Immediate gratification	Delayed gratification
Work certainty	Work uncertainty
Gainful employment	Underemployment & unemployment
Millennial & Gen-Z independence	Millennial & Gen-Z dependence on parents
Little school debt	$30K average school debt
Start family and purchase home by 30	Delay family and purchase of home
Work is local	Work is global
Disruption impacts local	Disruption impacts global and similar

FUTURE OF WORK

My second piece of advice is to stay global. As the world continues to change and we become more connected to each other, globalization will bring both benefits and disruptions to our lives. But either way, it's here, and it's not going away.
Barack Obama – U.S. President

The *Future of Work* may be as important and impactful change to people after climate change. Climate change is too distant. Work is too present. Let's explain this.

Climate change deals with the possibility of human extinction and seems far in the future. The *Future of Work* impacts people on a daily basis since it deals with our human needs, wants, and expectations. The *Future of Work* is now! So, we'd say that the *Future of Work* is important and relevant to the vast majority of people worldwide.

So, what's important about the *Future of Work*? McKinsey, the global consulting firm, estimates that between the present and 2030, 75 to 375 million workers need to switch jobs that will require new skills and new education just due to automation and tech disruption:

> "In terms of magnitude, it's akin to coping with the large-scale shift from agricultural work to manufacturing that occurred in the early 20th century in North America and Europe, and more recently in China. But in terms of who must find new jobs, we are moving into uncharted territory. Those earlier workforce transformations took place over many decades, allowing older workers to retire and new entrants to the workforce to transition to the growing industries. But the speed of change today is potentially faster. The task confronting every economy, particularly advanced economies, will likely be to retrain and redeploy tens of millions of midcareer, middle-age workers."[3]

Work Lesson Earned: The really bad news: Goldman Sachs estimates: "1/3 of the workforce will transfer to new occupations over the next five years".[4] So, are you future-ready? Pay attention to your *Future of Work*? Read this book. Take notes. Read up on what's happening to careers, jobs, and work. Listen to *Future of Work* podcasts, go to a seminar, and check if your skills are up-to-date.

WORKING IT CONTEXT!

The right questions don't change as often as the answers do.
Peter Drucker – Management Guru

In this book, we explore the *Future of Work* and how it's going to affect Vucans in critical ways. We look at **Disruption Rules** through the lens of paradigm shifts, disruptive forces, and VUCA (explained soon). We look at what causes these changes, why it matters to you the reader, how it impacts you, and most importantly, what you can learn and do as a result of these disruptions.

The main title of this book is **Working It**. As the title implies, **Working It** can be what you do to earn a living or what you do to have fun or how you live your life. In other words, **Working It** is all the stuff you do that have meaning and value for you. So when you go through this book, you'll notice that many of the stories go beyond what you do at the place that provides you income. We focus on the meaning and things that are important to your **Working It**.

When there's a disruption, most of us find a job or career book to find answers and encouragement. Most old-school job books provide life, career, or job road maps. Follow these steps and you'll get to where you want to be. If you believe these principles and follow these practices, you'll find a satisfying job and enjoy a substantial salary with guaranteed yearly increases. In this book, we want to get real, provide insights, and tell it like it is!

Working It is about dreams and managing expectations. The traditional work model assumed the next generation would be better off than the current generation. This is the conventional wisdom throughout the world. However, in many countries this is no longer the case. An overarching theme throughout this book is there are a fewer great opportunities for people with higher expectations and higher educations. Some things gotta give.

A friend of mine years ago said: 'Context is worth 20 IQ points'. Context provides clarity and understanding. In this section of the book, we provide the context on *the Future of Work*. We look at:

- How the *Future of Work* project started.
- 'Look and feel' of **Working It**: **Disruption Rules** book.
- How disruption rules.
- 7P's work framework and structure.

WORKING IT 'LOOK AND FEEL'

In a digital world, there are numerous technologies that we are attached to that create infinite interruption.

Tim Ferriss - Author

I'm a Gutenberg person. What do I mean? Well, I process information, in this case the written word, in a left-to-right, linear narrative. Each sentence has a thought that builds into the next sentence, paragraph, section, and chapter. The process builds on itself leading to insights, conclusions, and recommendations. Most of our communications, problem-solving, and decision-making are based on this linear model.

Most of us are evolving into digital immigrants. Let me explain. People growing up today, digital natives, seem to process information in almost a non-linear fashion. Several examples may clarify this. You've seen a music video? Powerful, kinetic images, gifs, memes, tropes, and language are flashed every several seconds. The Gutenbergs among us exclaim: 'say what'? Digital natives say: 'dope' - Google 'Urban Dictionary' for the online definition.

Digital natives convey and process digital information differently almost experientially. The Gutenbergs miss the meme, video, or gif experience because the images and lyrics don't seem to be connected and make little sense. I suppose it's a generational and contextual thing.

Another example may help. All of us surf the Web and lean in to certain content. The process is pretty simple. You click on a topic and it links you to another one. The connections between topics can be strong or loose. A link can even connect you to something purely random. The point is that you may learn this way. You develop an overall itch, passion, context, or perspective of a topic and if you want more detail, you drill down.

Work Lesson Earned: We've tried to capture a **Work Lesson Earned**™ in each story. We want to share replicable and scalable 'tips and tools' that hopefully can work for you in a disruptive work world. These 'tips and tools' can be both conventional as well as counterintuitive.

DO YOU KNOW TODAY'S WORK RULES?

Three Rules of Work: Out of clutter find simplicity. From discord find harmony. In the middle of difficulty lies opportunity.
Albert Einstein - Physicist

Work is described in terms of a set of changing 1. Rules; 2. Boundary conditions; 3. Tools, and 4. Expectations. Let's look at each: You think you know your work rules, because they were presented to you in a policy manual, workshop, or personal one-on-one. It was something like 'to get along, play along'. These policies and instructions may have worked for you. You knew what was expected and you learned how to do what was expected.

In the age of me-too, identity politics, and work tribes, do you *really* know your present work, career, and job rules; what is expected of you; what can be or can't be done; what can be discussed and said to whom and when; and what are the known and unspoken enhancers, enforcers, and forbidden rules at work? Companies and workers are struggling with these.

Until a few years ago, the boundary conditions for almost all businesses were the four walls in which work was conducted. It may have been the office, factory, restaurant, or some other workplace. With the virtual office, the workplace may be corporate headquarters, your home, remote, WeWork, no office, or even an automobile anywhere in the world.

The tools of the workplace not too many years ago were pens and mechanical devices. Now, workplace tools are digital including smart phones, RFID, VR, AR, voice recognition, artificial intelligence, algorithms, and big data. Are you current with the tools and techniques of your profession and work expectations? Millennials pride themselves knowing current workplace tools, however they know the tools as users not as developers. For example, do you code?

A person entering the workplace twenty or even ten years ago assumed loyalty to a company was rewarded with lifetime work. No longer! Employers make us responsible for our employability to develop value-adding skills. Do you know your company's, client's or boss's expectations?

Work Lesson Earned: Almost all work 1. Rules; 2. Boundary conditions; 3. Tools, and 4. Expectations have changed or are changing. In **Working It**, we discuss each. What new rules have impacted you the most? What do you fear the most?

WORKING IT: DISRUPTION RULES

Every single industry is going through a major business model and technology oriented disruption.
Aaron Levie - CEO of Box

Disruption Rules! Why did I use this in the **Working It** title? Good question! Think about the reboot button on electronics you own. What do you do? You punch a button and the machine goes back to its original state. You reboot to fix something that isn't working. You reboot to refresh, have a new start, or reinvent yourself. Work paradigms and rules are disrupted so companies and people are rebooting their work assumptions.

Everything seems to be changing. The marketplace is getting tougher. Companies are reassessing their business models, competitive assumptions, and even customer requirements. *Foreign Affairs* magazine expressed it well:

> "New technologies have been revolutionizing the world for centuries, transforming life and labor and enabling an extraordinary flourishing of human development. Now some argue that advances in automation and artificial intelligence are causing us to take yet another world-historical leap into the unknown."[5]

Workers are reassessing their marketability and employability. Work is harder for many. Workers search for meaning at work. Others simply want to have a livable wage. Hostilities among work tribes are increasing. Raises are often non-existent. Work is competitive. Personal life and work brands are adapting.

We want to respect the readers' personal work vision and work models. Many people are deciding not to work for traditional companies. They opt for gig, startup, or non-traditional work. This is great! What works for you is fine.

Work Lesson Earned: We want to provide you, the reader, with options in terms of providing new contexts; offering new opportunities; seeing what others can't; expanding your opportunity borders; redefining what work means to you; and providing new lens and frameworks by which to look at your work.

WORK LESSON EARNED™

In **Working It: Disruption Rules**, I've tried to blend a linear narrative with a non-linear approach. Each story is a block of information, a stand-alone thought-bite about work, career, and job disruption, that is distilled into a one-page story. While the thought bite may seem like fluffy popcorn, we hope it can provide bread crumbs for you to follow regarding your *Future of Work*.

The thought-bite may be loosely connected to the chapter and may not be a linear jump from the previous story. This was done intentionally. Why? You, the reader, can read this book from beginning-to-end (Gutenberg approach) or can dip into it as required to pick up thought-bites, noodle them, and then revisit them later on (digital approach).

Work Lesson Earned. We present one-page stories that walk and lead you through the changes of what we call the disruptions of work.

Caveat: Most work innovation and career success involves failure. Why failure? And, ultimate success requires risk acceptance and a high tolerance for failure. **Working It** emphasizes Risk-Based, Problem-Solving (RBPS) and Risk-Based, Decision-Making (RBDM) both are the essence of work success/failure, personal self-management, adding value, career resilience, execution, and career agility. Why RBPS and RBDM? Designing your future involves making conscious and smart choices. Future workers will do hybrid jobs involving pivoting and solving different problems. And, RBPS and RBDM ensure that you can be: proactive, preventive, predictive, and even preemptive™ in your work choices.

Work Lesson Earned: In each story, we capture a **Work Lesson Earned**, which is the distillation of **Working It**. Why? We wanted to flip the expression: Life Lesson Learned. Work is our focus, specifically our personal expression and adding market value. All life and work are lessons. It's up to us to learn from them. Then, we want to focus on things you've done and earned.

Caveat: **Work Lesson Earned** illustrates work context, considerations, assumptions, and impacts that may be valid for some readers and not for others. We want to state there's no guarantee the **Work Lesson Earned** will be relevant next month or are for all readers. This book simply provides guidelines that you must use with your professional discretion. Practice common sense and seek a workplace professional if you have any personal questions.

THIS IS MY STORY – WHAT'S YOURS?

Stories are the equipment of living.
Kenneth Burke – Historian

I started out of high school doing manual work. My first job was as an Ordinary Seaman in the Merchant Marine. I worked on rust bucket ships on and off for 5 years. This manual work was very hard and frankly not suited to my style, abilities, temperament, and life direction. Freighters now are on the way to be fully automated. In other words, no people on board.

Work Lesson Earned: These were my first big work lessons: Put food on the table. Try different things and different jobs. Find what you love to do. Develop an aptitude to do it well. Make sure that someone is willing to pay for it.

I then got a liberal arts degree in political science. Great! But, what was I going to do with a degree that pointed me to politics. Me - a libertarian. Go figure!

Work Lesson Earned: Have a vocation and an avocation. Your vocation is your portable meal ticket and your avocation is what you love to do but doesn't necessarily pay the rent or put food on the table. And, if you can blend your avocation with your vocation, you've been blessed.

Since I needed a vocation I migrated into oil/gas engineering in my mid-twenties. I became a licensed mechanical engineer. Great decision! Had loads of fun as an engineer designing and building things: oil terminals, high-pressure pipelines, and process facilities. Until the oil bust. Then, I couldn't get a job for my life. This was another huge lesson.

Work Lesson Earned: Things change so be prepared, be agile, and be resilient. I stayed in engineering but reengineered my career horizontally. I became proficient in mechanical, manufacturing, quality, supply management, software, cyber security, supply management, risk management, artificial intelligence, and industrial engineering. I even started writing books on these subjects. These geeky tomes were full of multi-syllabic words that were the identifying trademarks of engineering professionals. I learned I had the ability to glue words together.

Work Lesson Earned: Messages about inherent abilities come from unexpected quarters. So, listen carefully.

During this period of my portable career, I worked for a number of 'my way or the highway' bosses. This management style clanged with me. So I left big business to work as an entrepreneur for which I was totally unprepared. I had been trained, nurtured, promoted, and reinforced for geek abilities. During this state, I mostly had safe corporate homes, where I could homestead.

Work Lesson Earned: *Degeek.* Well, what do I mean? Entrepreneurship requires new business, life, and work skills. Technical abilities whether accounting, law, or engineering get a job done, but don't necessarily support entrepreneurship in terms of running a business, making payroll, or shaking the money tree (making a profit). I had to learn how to sell and schmooze - in others words I had to grow horizontally again and become a people-person.

How far should you go to degeek. Do what fits and make it work for you. I now build apps. I do AI. I architect business models. I disrupt verticals. However, I'm a neo - Luddite. I have an iPhone 3. I'm not on Facebook. I only use LinkedIn.

I've written about thirty or so books and designed/deployed lots of products. Some bombed. Some floated. And, one or two actually earned out. I've founded a number of businesses including 800.Compete.com, WorkingIt.com, WorkingIt.TV, QualityPlusEngineering.com, AsianChixWithAttitude.com, Greg's Outrageous Fortune Cookie Company, a publishing business, and loads of others. Some failed. Some did OK. Few did great.

Work Lesson Earned: The essence of **Working It** is captured in these **Work Lessons Earned**. Fail fast. Learn. Do, do, and do again. Learn from your mistakes then do things differently until you discover your own true magic. This book is my story. Your work story needs to take shape and be told. So, pay heed. Understand conventional and counter-intuitive work rules. Then, hack these rules so they work for you. Define what work success means to you. Have fun. Do good. Treat people fairly. This is our vision of **Working It: Disruption Rules**. What are yours going to be?

MOORE'S LAW AND YOUR WORK DISRUPTION

Because of the nature of Moore's law, anything that an extremely clever graphics programmer can do at one point can be replicated by a merely competent programmer
some number of years later.
John Carmack - Software Engineer

Number of years ago, several of us at IEEE wondered what are the people implications of what is commonly called Moore's Law.

Gordon Moore was one of the founders of Intel. Moore's Law states that the
number of transistors that can fit into a computer chip doubles every 18 months
to two years. Moore's Law expanded to include any area dealing with tech
where the rate of change about doubles in two years or costs half as much. The
list of technologies that now follow Moore's Law include self-driving cars, 3-D
printing, robotics, VR, gene editing, and the Internet of Things. As the title of
this book says: Moore's Law is synonymous with **Disruption Rules**.

So, we wondered what would happen if Moore's Law applied to people: to engineers and IT professionals where the amount of knowledge in a domain may
double in four years or less. No easy answer! Why? Well, it's complicated.

So, a specific thought experiment may help. We wondered what would happen
to a person graduating from Stanford with a degree in Computer Science or
Electrical Engineering with a specialty in a bleeding edge domain such as in
cyber security, robotics, artificial intelligence, machine learning, nanotechnol-
ogy, and many other tech disciplines. So let's see, the engineer is 22 at graduation. By the time she's 26, knowledge in the field has doubled. Eight years after
graduation, knowledge in the field has quadrupled. Anyway you get the idea.
What would happen to her marketability and employability because knowledge
in the field had increased fourfold by the time she was 30 and she hadn't upgraded her engineering?

Work Lesson Earned: The premise of **Working It: Disruption Rules** is we now
are ALL techies. Our careers and jobs will follow Moore's law. YOU now are the
thought experiment. How will Moore's law impact you? You'll have to adopt
new behaviors, be resilient, and learn new skills. For example, artificial intelligence, robotics, and automation will impact YOU – either in a minor way of
changing your work or a major way even displacing you This is OUR *Future of
Work* where changing tech drives obsolescence.

7P'S WORK FRAMEWORK

You don't have to be a genius or a visionary or even a college graduate to be successful. You just need a framework and a dream.
Michael Dell - Founder of Dell Computers

A full treatment of work, careers, and jobs is beyond the scope of this book and frankly beyond my abilities. **Working It: Disruption Rules** offers a unique structure, framework, and lens for your *Future of Work* .

Expressed another way, **Working It** offers a structure for understanding and a framework for looking at your work, career, and job. **Working It** is not the total answer. Hopefully, it offers glimpses of what's occurring around you whether you work for someone or for yourself or are exploring options.

One of the powerful analytical tools in management theory is the systems approach that explains complex relationships in simple terms. **Working It: Disruption Rules** presents a systems approach to work. Elements of a system can be parts of a machine, actors in a play, or people at work.

In this book, our 7P work system, framework, or architecture consists of Paradigms, People, Principles, Practices, Products, Processes, and Projects®. Why did I use the 7P's structure? It's lucky seven. Yes, I know that's a shallow answer. It's mnemonic. It explains many work disruptions and how your career may develop.

In this edition of the **Working It**, we're emphasizing 3 additional P's: passion, purpose, and profit. Why? Passion is not only the desire to do (execute) the work, but goes beyond the required and desired - to move into the innovation zone. Purpose is the desire to be one with your work, to have a personal connection with the value and calling of your work. And of course, profit or a performance metric is required to ensure your journey is in the right direction, speed, and destination. Companies and startups are not philanthropies as many would like to believe.

Work Lesson Earned: We hope **Working It** can provide you, the reader, with a way to assess your work based on the 7P attributes: Paradigms, People, Principles, Practices, Products, Processes, and Projects®. As well, we hope to provide context, guidance, direction, tools and tips for dealing with disruption. Finally, we hope the 7P's become part of your life story and work narrative.

WHAT ARE THE 7P'S®?

Work is changing. And in the future, the nature of work may look drastically different.
Boston NPR Station

Work and careers follow a cycle. The numbers are stunning. What does U.S. Department of Labor say? We'll have 5/6/7 careers in our lifetime. That's phenomenal. The average job tenure is going to be 2/3 years. That means that each 2/3 years, we'll move on to a new career that may be an extension of the present one or a completely new career opportunity. What drives each cycle? Globalization. Politics. Recessions. New business paradigms. New business models. Tech drivers. Outsourcing. Offshoring. Financial cataclysms. Climate change.

We liked the 4P's architecture of Marketing: Product, Price, Place, and Promotion. We felt that work could be subsumed under our 7P's framework, much like marketing's 4P's.

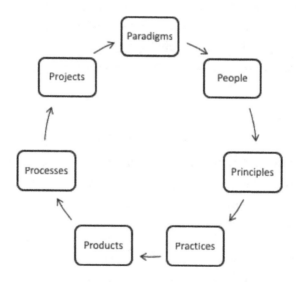

When there's a major, systemic disruption in the economy or in one's vertical (industry sector), a person may lose his/her job and look for a new one. Alternatively, the disruption may be driven by personal circumstances or personal decisions. However, every time a person goes through one of these changes, the 7P's cycle or wheel starts again.

The cycle means that you have to understand the shifting Paradigms that are changing work; review the People element (how will the loss of work or a new job impact your family, etc).; understand how your Principles and those of the company match; learn new skills and develop new Practices; develop your personal brand (Product); learn new Processes or ways of working; and taskify and Projectize your work. So in each chapter of this book, you'll discover:

PARADIGMS

Globalism, workism, off shoring, outsourcing, competitiveness, artificial intelligence, automation, identity politics, and tech will create new work, career, and job paradigms. So, what do you think organizations and work will look like after these paradigm shifts?

Predictions are made on quicksand because once they're made, things change again. In **Working It: Disruption Rules**, we'll introduce the significant shifting work paradigms, artificial intelligence and how they will redefine organizations, their business models, and the fundamentals of work. These shifting paradigms will introduce changes that will deeply impact how your work is done, who has work, and how you'll interact with your co-workers and even buddy machines (cobots).

PEOPLE

Remember, work is all about people! Sometimes, it's forgotten that people make an organization. People make critical buy and sell decisions. People develop new products. People service other people. People consume products and services. Without people, there are no customers, no consumers, no organizations, and no reason for work.

And when the paradigm shift or disruption occurs, people will always be blindsided. They won't see it because they're in the box and can't see the warping occurring in their work box.

PRINCIPLES

What's your employer's vision and mission? What's your personal vision and purpose? Are your employer's mission and yours aligned? Let's first start with your employer. Should a business steward its resources for the benefit of future generations, share them with its workers, or maximize immediate financial returns for its shareholders?

And, what's your fundamental purpose for working? Should your passions and principles be aligned with those of your employer, partners, and others? What should you do if there's little alignment? Or, what should you do when the thrill is gone from a job or career? Or, what should you do if you can't move up? Accept the conditions, move on, or start your own business? We'll discuss these all-important questions.

PRACTICES
There are self-management practices that can spell success in your work, career, and job. Self-management is all about self-empowerment through self-control, specifically learning how to manage customer, time, quality, communications, risk, tech, and performance commitments, which are critical work practices.

Let's look at one practice. Everyone is now a techie. Tech is both the biggest driver and facilitator of workplace disruption. Tech creates boundaryless companies, which results in flat hierarchies and boundaryless careers. Where a career was once a vertical progression in a company, it's now the accumulation and implementation of value-added practices, information, and knowledge gained through diverse work experiences.

PRODUCTS
While it may sound callous, we're all products or brands that offer value to a buyer. Each of us needs to develop and distill our value-added differentiators. We're hearing buzz about the concept of Me-Inc. or Brand You, where each one of us either as a full time employee or independent contractor is essentially a value-adding, small business with products and services.

PROCESSES
A company's core processes is its business model - how it conducts its business or in other words, how it works day-in and day-out. These core processes are the basic building blocks and value-adding activities of a business. They may be 'world class' intellectual property (IP), activities, policies, systems, people, etc.

They differentiate a company from its competition. They provide high customer satisfaction and generate income opportunities.

In much the same way, each of us has a bundle of value-adding processes involving personal knowledge, practices, skills, and competencies. These core proficiencies are what you can monetize as side-hustles or sell to organizations to develop and monetize.

PROJECTS

Work and side-hustles are organized around projects. Project management is evolving into a critical self-management skill to ensure the right work is done right on time and within budget. These activities must be accomplished quickly, effectively, and efficiently. A project may involve typing a letter, responding to a customer request, developing a killer app, or putting a person on the moon.

Eighty percent of the work in an organization may be project based. Organizations are going as far as projectizing all their activities including their core processes. Many creative, consulting, engineering, and medical offices are already 100% projectized. When customer expectations are sky high and competition is deadly, the conventional wisdom is that projectized teams differentiate winners from losers.

Work Lesson Earned: This is my stream of consciousness around the *Future of Work*. I've listened and curated many workplace conversations and placed them in the 7P's framework. Do I have all the answers on work? No! However, I do want you to ask critical questions about the *Future of Work* and encourage new thinking of your *Future of Work*. Work is disrupted throughout the world. And hopefully, **Working It** can be your platform to understand and adapt to it.

JUST THE FACTS OR LEAST MY INTERPRETATION OF THEM

All truth passes through three stages. First, it is ridiculed. Second, it is violently opposed. Third, it is accepted as being self-evident.
Arthur Schopenhauer - Philosopher

I really can't understand the lack of truth and candor from our political and business leaders. I don't know if they're lying (commission) or deceiving (omission) or simply aspirational (dreaming). My goal in **Working It** is to share the truth of **Disruption Rules** – or at least my sense of the truth – about work, your career, and your job.

All companies are asking tough questions and making hard risk-based decisions on where to go, how to get there, and how to make margin (profit). But, you'll be reading about the *Future of Work* and its direction from how company executives and consultants want you to see it. You may disagree with what I say and how I say it. However, a hard-nosed approach of the *Future of Work* is prevalent in many companies. The *Wall Street Journal* reported:

> "By taking a knife to the (Goldman Sachs Group) business, Mr. Solomon (CEO) is sending a message down the ranks that nothing is sacred."[6]

Question arises? 'Why won't company or government executives tell you the truth?' Well, it's spelled 'litigation' or 'reputational risk'. They don't want to go to court. They don't want to breach any laws. They don't want to be fired prematurely. They don't want to be 'me-too'ed'. Let's call it their due diligence to keep their jobs. Is this deception? Maybe. Most executives and managers in a candid, but not attributable moment will say it's self-preservation.

Question arises? 'Why don't our politicians tell you the truth'? As my daughter used to say: 'This is a double duh'. Humanist reviewers may feel that this book may be a little brutal. What about following your life's bliss or calling? Do what you love! Socialism may be the answer. This is great if you can make it happen. I believe that we're moving to a disruptive, risk-based, and data-driven work environment. It is more head, than heart or gut.

Work Lesson Earned: In **Working It**, we explore the big questions of work, careers, and jobs. The truth can hurt. However, I hope and pray my sense of the truth can set you free. Enjoy. If you want to contact me, email me at: **GregH@Europa.com**. We'd like to hear your thoughts.

PARADIGMS

-

DISRUPTION
IN VUCA WORLD
IN VUCA TIME

This element of the 7P's framework deals with Paradigms. Paradigms focus on the disruptive shifts in government, companies, professions and people. Joel Barker in **Paradigms: The Business of Discovering the Future** defined a paradigm as:

> ... "set of rules and regulations (written or unwritten) that does two things: 1. It establishes or defines boundaries; and 2. It tells you how to behave inside the boundaries in order to be successful."[7]

The **Working It** subtitle is **Disruption Rules**. It pretty much frames the discussion around the *Future of Work*. So in this section, we focus on how paradigm shifts including how artificial intelligence and automation will disrupt work, business models, and professions. We discuss new work rules and regulations, new boundary conditions, and changes in work, jobs, and businesses.

Paradigm shifts create both disruption and risks. In this book, we look at risks in terms of two components: 1. Downside consequence and 2. Upside opportunity. While most of us focus on the former, the latter drives change, innovation, value, and growth.

VUCAN DRIVERS - PARADIGMS

Old School	New School
Static paradigms	Shifting paradigms
Stable career and work paradigms	Disruptive career and work paradigms
Static world and paradigms	VUCA world and shifting paradigms
Sequential time	VUCA time
We are all 'normals'	We are all 'Vucans'
Local environmental degradation	Global warming
Human evolution	Human extinction
Static or incremental tech	Disruptive tech
Brick and mortar shrinkage	Online retail expansion
Situational anxiety	Disruptive social anxiety
Lifelong employment	Just-in-time work requiring new skills
Static and rules based, artificial intelligence	Self-learning and adapting artificial intelligence
Capitalist system	Capitalist, socialist and organic systems
Capitalist work world	Orange, Green and Blue work worlds
On campus education model	Online, MOOC, and innovative education models
Brick & mortar offices	Pop up offices
Brick & mortar companies with full time workers	Digital companies with ghost workers
External drivers to adaptation	External and internal drivers to adaptation and self-disruption
Security	Insecurity
Climate change denial	Climate change acceptance
Simple questions and answers	Difficult questions with few if any simple answers
Acceptance	Desire for change
4G	5G
Steady-state professions	Disrupted & disappearing professions

PARADIGMS @ RISK

Paradigm: Provides us a language, a common set of assumptions, and a common set of expectations of what may occur in the future.
Joel Barker - Author

Paradigms are rules. Current work, business, and personal paradigms have shifted in unexpected and radical ways. Let's look at the word a little closer. The root of paradigm comes from the Greek and means a pattern, model, or rule. A paradigm is the way or pattern you perceive your world. It can mean a world of difference. Fish perceive their world through water. People perceive their world through air. People perceive their value and principles through work.

Paradigm shifts foreshadow larger changes in work rules. What was the right thing to do before may now be wrong? What was the pathway to career success may now be different. What was expressly acceptable may now be forbidden workplace behavior. These shifts are difficult for people who were hired, taught, recognized, promoted, and reinforced for a set of behaviors and skills that are now either unacceptable or have radically changed.

New paradigms destroy the existing rules and create a new order or set of rules. Today's killer idea is tomorrow's has been. The old idea, principle, process, system, belief, app, or product is trashed because it's too difficult to implement, it costs too much to implement, people don't understand it, or for a host of other reasons. Your perception of success, worth, and confidence of who you are, what you do, and how you work may change.

The classic example is the buggy whip industry totally disappeared along with carriages as the automobile became the favored method for moving people. Autonomous vehicles (robot driven) in 5 to 10 years may do the same for driven vehicles.

Work Lesson Earned: Start understanding the paradigms that affect your company, clients, and work. If you want to stay employed, know what drives your company or client and know what keeps executives up at night. I'm surprised how many workers and contractors don't know their company's or client's business models. I ask in our workshops: 'Who knows your company's business model'? I'm usually shocked. About 10% do. Not good!

WE'RE ALL VUCANS NOW!

In business, the VUCA world is the culmination of 50 years of movement from an industrial to an information economy.
Deloitte – Consulting Firm

We're all Vucans now! Why? We live in a VUCA world in VUCA time. VUCA stands for Volatility, Uncertainty, Complexity, and Ambiguity. Not too sure what this means? Take a look at any news broadcast or front page of any national newspaper. It's all about VUCA that puts all work @ risk.

What's causing these paradigm shifts? Many of the business stories and personal narratives in this book deal with VUCA. Let's look at each VUCA element:

- **Volatility:** Volatility is the tendency of what appears as normal situations can change quickly and unpredictably into unusual, unexpected, and even unimaginable situations. For example, the unexpected or even 100-year events seem to be occurring more frequently and have unexpected consequences.   Who would have expected repeated tsunamis, wild fires, heat, floods, tornados, hurricanes, and the list goes on?
- **Uncertainty:** Uncertainty is the inability to understand of what's going on around us, that breeds mistrust. For example, who would expect government shutdowns, trade wars with neighbors, digital iron curtain disputes with China, and well-known companies going bust?
- **Complexity:** New business models, systems, processes, apps, products, and social interactions are complex. For example, problems are so complex with many interacting variables, that solutions and even agreement can't be found.
- **Ambiguity:** Issues that should be straight forward and solvable are now ambiguous and cloudy as seen through different lens. In the new normal, business rules, social identity, and political rules are not clear, misinterpreted, and even unresolvable. There's a higher potential of misreads due to lack of good information and too much VUCA. Business decisions that should be based on a clear cause and effect relationship seem to be irreconcilable.

Work Lesson Earned: The logic flow in this book is pretty straight forward: VUCA => Paradigm Shifts => Disruption => Risk=> RBPS/RBDM.   While most of the examples in this book deal with U.S. examples. VUCA is occurring worldwide in all companies and we're now all Vucans (VUCA people).

CHRISTENSEN: DISRUPTION GURU

Breaking an old business model is always going to require leaders to follow their instincts. There will always be persuasive reasons not to take a risk. But if you only do what worked in the past, you'll wake up one day and find that you've been passed by. **Clayton Christensen – Disruption Theorist and Writer**

Clayton Christensen is the current guru and popularizer of business and personal disruption. His pattern of business disruption is all too familiar.

Competitors with new platforms and new business models enter a market because they see opportunities to make money, satisfy customers effectively, or make a difference if they are a non-profit. The startup or disrupter starts by developing lower cost or lower quality products or services but at an acceptable price to the customer. Or, the startup offers an innovative app, product, or service. These apps, products, or services capture the customer's attention and eventually gain market share. These innovative products, and services are eventually tweaked and improved so the startup can go up-market.

So, what happens to existing companies? Existing companies choose to ignore or dismiss these startups. Big companies will say: 'we're big and smart'; 'the entrant is stupid and can't scale'; or even 'this too shall pass'. Or, there may be other excuses and rationalizations.

Existing firms continue to pursue their higher margin, high-quality, branded, and high-volume business. Over time, the startup disruptor achieves an acceptable quality level to a niche segment and then to a much broader part of market. This way, the startup begins to gain traction and begins to compete with existing companies.

Work Lesson Earned: If you're a small business owner, professional service firm, or contractor, pay special attention to the Christensen disruption model. If you're an employee of one of these large existing companies, be aware. Acknowledge your old 'is' has changed and now you need to deal with the 'as is' or what 'can be' of your new work, career, and job realities. Even things that were iron-clad promises such as promotions, work, and even pensions may disappear in the blink of an eye. Companies owe you nothing!

CLIMATE DISRUPTION – GLOBAL EXTINCTION

Is climate change humanity's greatest ever risk management failure?
The Guardian newspaper

Climate change. Global warming. These are the 'new normal' or the ultimate 'Horsemen of the Apocalypse'. U.S. intelligence said:

> "Global environmental and ecological degradation, as well as climate change, are likely to fuel competition for resources, economic distress, and social discontent through 2019 and beyond. Climate hazards such as extreme weather, higher temperatures, droughts, floods, wildfires, storms, sea level rise, soil degradation, and acidifying oceans are intensifying, threatening infrastructure, health, and water and food security."[8]

Risk likelihood as well as direct risk consequences are increasing. Extreme heat is impacting global food supplies, all supply chains, housing near the ocean, increases in cancer, and many other factors. Are you a denier? According to a recent report, there's 95% likelihood that people are the drivers of climate change through carbon dioxide emission.[9] OK, is human extinction too strong of a prediction? The *New York Times* and U.N. say pretty much the same:

> "Humans are transforming Earth's natural landscapes so dramatically that as many as one million plant and animal species are now at risk of extinction, posing a dire threat to ecosystems that people all over the world depend on for their survival, a sweeping new United Nations assessment has concluded."[10]

You may be a green believer or even an evangelist. Or, you may be a heretic. It really doesn't matter. We're in a heating global environmental and a changing political environment. So, pay attention to sustainability. I was a green skeptic until I saw first-hand major environmental changes occurring over a few years. I fish for salmon on the Columbia River in Oregon, USA., which is a beautiful and pristine environment. The problem is that over the last 30 years, salmon fishing changed. Fewer fish. Smaller fish. Not good. As an engineer, I thought that we were going through a macro weather cycle from warm to cold.

Work Lessons Learned: So, what does this have to do with your work? As traditional industries adapt to the changing environment, consider working in emerging green businesses to save human kind. You're having fun. You're doing good. You're saving the planet.

TECH DISRUPTION EATS COMPANIES

Over the next 10 years, I expect many more industries to be disrupted by software, with new world-beating Silicon Valley companies doing the disruption in more cases than not.

Marc Andreessen - Entrepreneur

We've been involved in engineering and tech automation for many years. What surprises us is the observable breadth, depth, and impacts of automation over the last five years.

So, what's the big deal about automation? "Automation exists to substitute work undertaken by humans with work done by machines, with the aim of increasing the quality and quantity of output at a reduced cost."[11] So, what happens to people and workers? What happens to high paying work?

That pretty much says it all! Automation disrupts business and displaces Vucans. Automation stories are rising in the U.S., China, India, and all parts of the world. For example, one of China's big e-commerce companies, has a warehouse in Shanghai where 4 engineers service all the robots in a mega fulfillment center. Amazon has an army of 100,000 robots that displace humans. So, what happens to Vucans? We're just beginning to see and understand social impacts.

Automation is accelerating. Over the past few years, most if not all established and legacy companies realize they must transform their 'brick and mortar' business models to online and automated models to thrive or even just survive.

Work Lesson Earned: You say: 'So what? This won't affect me.' Years ago, Xerox PARC CEO Stephen Hoover said: "Every company is a tech company". This was prescient because it's now true.

SURREAL TECH DIFFUSION

It's not the big (fish) that eat the small (fish), it's the fast (fish) that eat the slow (fish).
Jason Jennings – Author

In real estate, it's all about location … location … location. In VUCA life and work, it's all about time … time … time. It's about your smart choices (RBPS & RBDM) – how you decide to use limited time, resources, and money. It's about innovating and surviving disruption through smart problem-solving and decision-making. You can't be all things to all people. So, time or specifically the lack of it is increasing anxiety.

Disruption changes our understanding of time. Things gotta get done faster. On budget. Within scope. With high quality. The below chart illustrates the tech diffusion model of the time to reach 50 million users.

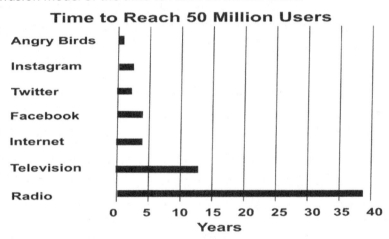

Forbes Magazine called time or specifically the lack of it "the biggest issue of our age". Time is fast, seamless, and almost instantaneous. Response times are squeezed to seize business opportunities or surpass competitors. Hyper global competition is the new normal. Competition done well results in high valued employment. Competition done poorly results in a race to the bottom. Time management is a business as well as a personal issue. Personal time management is fundamentally about life and work management.

Work Lesson Earned: It's all about focusing on what matters, on the Vucans impacting your life and the practices simplifying your life. It all comes down to making the right choices and controlling time to get the right things done right so that the critical people in your life are satisfied.

ARTIFICIAL INTELLIGENCE EATS JOBS

I think we should be very careful about artificial intelligence. If I had to guess at what our biggest existential threat is, it's probably that. So we need to be very careful.
Elon Musk - Entrepreneur

Artificial intelligence and robots conjure up images of killer robots much like the Terminator movie. So, Elon Musk, founder of Tesla, warns:

> "With artificial intelligence we are summoning the demon. In all those stories where there's the guy with the pentagram and the holy water, it's like – yeah, he's sure he can control the demon. Doesn't work out."[12]

Welding and pick/place factory robots have been around for 30 years. Commercial and collaborative robots are coming. Autonomous commercial robots on the street can deliver food. Autonomous drones in the air can deliver packages. Collaborative robots or cobots at work help us solve problems and make tough decisions. Personal robots at home answer our questions and manage our homes. So, robots are here! What now?

Let's look specifically at personal robots. They have come a long way out of the factory into our homes. They talk to us in simple terms. They clean carpets. They help us select music, book flights, control homes, lock doors, buy things, and help order our lives. What's next? Siri and Alexa for workplaces? Think of Amazon's Alexa or Apple's Siri solving your technical problems and autonomously making hard decisions.

How will Vucans and machines work together to solve problems and make decisions. The rules of engagement between Vucans and machines have not been determined. There are things the machines can do well. There are things that Vucans can do well.

Work Lesson Earned: Machines are getting smarter and humanlike. How did this happen? Smarter software. Faster processing. Better sensors. Human-like smarts. Worst case, put all of these together - you may have the start of robo – geddon – whatever that may mean?

EATING VUCANS

Disruption is, at its core, a really powerful idea, but everyone hijacks the idea to do whatever they want now.
Clayton Christensen - Author

Tech is eating Millennials since many seem anxious and angry. Millennials are the largest demographic segment in the U.S. and in many countries. This population cohort includes Vucans born between 1980 and 2000. In the U.S., there are 75 million Millennials. The median job tenure of workers ages 20 to 24 is less than 16 months.

Life and work are tough for the Millennial generation. In the U.S., they are saddled with college debt, about a 1/3 live at home, are reluctant to marry, and can't afford to purchase a home. The following quote from The *School of Life* seems to capture Millennial angst in the U.K and U.S.:

> "All of us worry to some degree. But for many, the worry is constant and all-consuming. We don't just worry about the gas bill, or the bin schedule. We worry that our friends secretly hate us; that we'll be abruptly fired from our jobs; that our partners are planning on leaving us for good. Catastrophe is not a remote possibility but an inevitability - a matter of when, not if."[13]

Millennial work angst is just as high. *Wall Street Journal* offered this perspective on college grads in 2019:

> "Gone are the days when new hires spent years learning the ropes before being handed important work. Today's graduates will be expected to jump right in."[14] And, if they don't stay on the job, bosses don't want to coach or mentor new talent.[15]

Work Lesson Earned: Are the above descriptions real for Millennials and most workers? Or, is it projection? Millennial workers globally seem anxious, angry, and resentful. This is a worldwide phenomenon where many Vucans have invested in education thinking that it was the meal ticket and passage to the good life. These expectations have not been met for large swathes of today's workers. And, here's the social conundrum. This global phenomenon has instilled stark fear into the world's plutocrats, 1-percenters, oligarchs, and haves. Many believe that socialism, social disruption, and class war may result because of disparities in income and lack of opportunities. What do you think?

END OF BUSINESS AS WE KNOW IT!

Every industry and every organization will have to transform itself in the next few years, in multiple ways, or fade away.
Tim O'Reilly - Founder of O'Reilly Publishing

VUCA, disruption, and risk are themes woven throughout this book. So for legacy companies, it's the end of business as they know it. Large company business models are disrupted by small agile companies with new ideas and new technologies. Startups develop simple solutions that can satisfy real needs faster, better, and more cheaply.

Many small businesses are not hiring. Let's look at retail disruption or what's called retail apocalypse. Think of the brick and mortar store that anchored your mall. The store and mall had massive fixed costs. The store had legions of workers.

Drive down any street. Retail store fronts are empty and have morphed into mobile retail trucks. Almost every type of small business with a brick-and-mortar location can morph into a truck offering mobile, specialized services such as food, house cleaning, food delivery, and almost any type of personalized service. The new truck stores are able to give customers flexible, just-in-time service at the right, profitable price. These businesses on wheels can tailor services to a particular market and customer segment. Tech has lowered the barriers of entry so that almost anyone can develop a replicable and scalable truck business. Unfortunately, these mobile stores hire few workers.

These small companies are called ankle biters. They are the biggest challenge to legacy (old-time) companies that have massive fixed costs, pre-existing structure, unchanging culture, calcified management attitudes, few innovative products, and workers with full benefits. The last item is great, but is less common.

Work Lesson Earned: Legacy companies ridicule, ignore, or are unaware of competitive startups. Established companies are often fossilized and can't adapt due to their internal systems and processes that reinforce the status quo. Internal change, self-disruption, and innovation are frowned upon. Internal management says 'this too shall pass'. The incumbents either are not able or unwilling to innovate and by the time they realize the need to adapt it's too late. Think of the countless retail shops that have closed in your neighborhood.

END OF COMPANIES AS WE KNOW THEM!

The system is not working. That is how a paradigm shift begins: the established way of seeing the world no longer functions.
Matthew Fox - American Actor

It's the end of companies as we know them.

It started with Joseph Schumpeter, who was the original voice of creative destruction early in the 20th century. Capitalism was evolving. Tech was growing. New businesses were spreading throughout the world. Schumpeter saw that capitalism inherently brought social, political, and economic disruption.

Almost a 100 years later, creative destruction is accelerating. Companies have to reinvent themselves based upon their context, regulatory requirements, competitive pressures, and customer requirements.

There's a visceral sense of urgency and even fear to be vigilant. The winners in this competition feel continuous pressure to self-disrupt to maintain their competitiveness. What are companies doing? Business models change. Processes are redesigned. Products and services are individualized. Services are developed and delivered in a just-in-time basis. Automation is everywhere.

Let's look a few industries that have been disrupted: mechanical watch, buggy whip, automotive manufacturing, Yellow Book publishing, high tech manufacturing, banking, real estate, newspapers, communications, publishing, and all retail.

Let's look at paradigm shifts in the automotive sector. Toyota Motor company President Akio Toyoda: "The automotive industry is now hurtling into an era of profound transformation, the likes of which come only once every 100 years."[16]

Work Lesson Earned: If you work for a company with obsolescent ideas, processes, apps, and products, it's time to analyze your work risks. Ask yourself: What are the likelihood and consequences of your company or client losing its competitive position and becoming a buggy whip company'? How are you going to be impacted? What are your contingency plans, your Plan B's and C's?

END OF EDUCATION AS WE KNOW IT!

10% of U.S. jobs will be lost to automation in 2019.
Forrester Research

A Millennial the other day was wearing a Y hoodie from Yale University his alma mater. We got into a conversation about work and what he was doing. Well, he was working for Amazon distribution center with a ¼ million dollar degree. Huh!

There has been a global and collective obsession with getting a college degree, seemingly regardless of its value and employability. The common perception based on historical numbers is that college graduates regardless of the degree make more over a lifetime than those without a degree.

Is this still true? Many Vucans are getting degrees with seemingly few employment opportunities. The result is many college graduates are underemployed or even unemployed. In 2019, University of Oregon graduated more than 700 people in Journalism and Communication – a dying profession.

Another obsession is the brand degree. So, would you rather go to Yale or State U is a question that came up with our 19 year old daughter. Millions of kids and parents in every country face this dilemma. Every country has its prestige and state (think value) universities. The former are expensive and the latter are relatively inexpensive.

The critical risk-based decision is: 'what's the better option for employability a ¼ million dollar degree from Harvard or Yale in German literature or an engineering degree from a State University'? Studies say: 'No'. There's a starting $39,000 difference in earnings between the highest and lowest paying college majors. "Where you go doesn't matter so much anymore, it matters what you take (degree)" was the conclusion.[17] You can get an online technical degree for 1/5 the cost of a prestigious university that offers more employability and lifetime marketability.

Work Lesson Earned: So, what are the takeaways? The privileged are fearful for their kid's employability. As cheating scandals indicate, the privileged will go to great lengths to secure life and work success for their kids. College branding counts less. Learning quickly may be the ultimate work differentiator.

END OF HR AS WE KNOW IT!

Self-disruption is akin to undergoing major surgery, but you are the one holding the scalpel.

Jay Samit – Entrepreneur

When it's your time, how are you going to survive and prosper from the digital disruption? Haven't thought about it? Here's a story that's going to impact all professions and functions.

Let's look at the Human Resource (HR) function. You'd think that people will always need to be recruited, hired, trained, promoted, and fired. This is what we'd call the 'full employment act' for HR professionals. But, guess again. IBM is using Artificial Intelligence (AI) to predict when and which workers will leave in the next six months with 95% accuracy. Show me a HR professional that can do this? The result is IBM has reduced its HR footprint and department by 30%.[18] And, this is only the beginning with all professions and functions.

It's estimated that 90% of big businesses have, are, or will be transforming their processes. A radical transformation may ensue if the customer is very unhappy with a product and may litigate because of health, safety, or environmental concerns. Or, the customer is simply unhappy with performance or product quality. Or, a company doesn't stand out from its competition. Or, a startup is transforming the current business model. In all these cases, a legacy company has to self-disrupt how it does business.

Only several years ago, there had to be a compelling reason or driver to transform an organization. Well, a critical message of **Working It** is that continual adaptation has been institutionalized and is part of the competitive landscape. Companies are continuously evaluating operations and readjusting them to add value, cut waste, lower costs, and improve quality. It may involve continuous, incremental improvement, or a radical transformation.

Work Lesson Earned: Surviving and prospering organizational transformations will be one of the toughest things you'll ever do. So, present yourself as a problem solver and part of the solution, not part of the problem.

END OF JOBS AS WE KNOW THEM!

Eighty-five (85%) of the jobs today's students will be doing in 2030 haven't been invented yet.

Institute for the Future

I've seen the *Future of Work*. And, I don't like it. Why? In Portland Oregon, a retail store sells kombucha, a slightly alcoholic green or black tea. Great location. Great storefront. Sure money maker! But, why don't I like it?

Look through the store window. Lots of customers are sitting at tables trying and sipping kombucha. So, we decided to go in and partake. Can't get in. We needed to swipe a card to unlock the door. We get in, look around and can't find any service person to place an order. Huh? A customer says: 'it's self-serve'. OK. Customers and no help. The entire shop was automated. No workers. Is this the future of bars, restaurants, and retail? May be. A recent report said that 70% of 'first jobs' such as retail are automatable.

The fear of massive job losses started about six years ago when University of Oxford released a report of job losses due to automation. The university reported that 47% of current U.S. jobs are at risk being impacted by or totally displaced by automation and artificial intelligence in 20 years or less.[19] In the latest report from Oxford, the numbers got worse, OK a lot worse - 80% of jobs in retail, transportation warehousing, and logistics are at risk and 63% of sales jobs are at risk. And by the way, the job losses and changes NOW will happen in 5 to 10 years or even less time.

Work Lesson Earned: The automation of work is a global challenge. There are not enough high paying jobs for Vucans and specifically recent college graduates. Millennial and Gen Z generations have been indoctrinated into believing that their economic future is guaranteed with any college education. The global reality is many recent college graduates are unemployed and/or underemployed as well as many older workers. The fear is real! The number of unemployed and/or underemployed college graduates can range from 40% to 60% in many countries. Hong Kong riots by highly educated Chinese is caused by lack of opportunities. This could be a cauldron of social unrest if these expectations and desires are not fulfilled.

END OF CITIES AS WE KNOW THEM!

Location. Location. Location. Every country wants to generate its own Silicon Valley. Why? Silicon Valley (S.V.) is a metaphor for generating new ideas, disruptive companies, killer products, and high value jobs.

Portland has Silicon Forest. Berlin has Silicon Alley. Dublin has Silicon Docks. They are mostly similar. So. let's unpack global S.V. in terms of the 7P's:

- **Paradigms:** Work messaging from S.V. include: Dream globally. Think innovatively. Do effectively. Live differently. Work disruptively. These are the mantras of Silicon Valley startups to disrupt the world.
- **People:** S.V. is a dream, the center of the tech universe, where breakthrough ideas flourish, geeks rule, new ideas disrupt the marketplace, and millions of lives are improved. And for the lucky few founders, billions are made.
- **Principles:** The principle of S.V. is to fail fast and fail often. In most companies and most countries, failure leads to shame, stigma, and unemployment. In S.V., lessons earned from failure is a badge of honor. The freedom to dream and fail tends to be strongly correlated to the ability to succeed and disrupt. Many countries carry a greater stigma of failure or bankruptcy which tend to be punitive.[20]
- **Practices:** So what made S.V. the dream capital of the world? Silicon Valley has great universities, innovative practices, startup culture, culture of risk-based problem-solving, wealthy investors, and history of garage startups that leveraged to be the world's biggest companies.
- **Products:** S.V.'s products and services have been so successful that countries want to replicate the dream in the hope of developing killer products, apps, and jobs.
- **Processes:** S.V. business models and innovative processes are adopted by countries and companies. S.V. has evolved into work style. WeWork offers community learning, working, and living. Work hustle is the new work gospel. Hustlemania is the personal 996 success model in China – not 9 to 5 like the U.S. but 9 am to 9 pm 6 days a week.
- **Projects:** Individual work is project based, lean, agile, and task oriented. Pull enough of these gigs together, you have a career with freedom.

Work Lesson Earned: The S.V. work model is an aspiring model. So, use the 7P's to unpack and develop your personal work model.

ARE YOU WORKING FOR THE NEXT GHOST COMPANY?

Let's go back a few years. In 1962 General Motors was one of the top five U.S. companies in terms of its market capitalization. GM at the time employed 500,000 high-wage, factory workers. Now, grocery chain Kroger employs around 400,000 low-wage workers. Target employs almost 350,000 workers. What's common among these companies is these jobs have high turnover, few benefits, and relatively low-wages. What's happened? High-wage jobs have moved to tech companies offering sky-high wages and long-term benefits.[21]

Let's look at tech companies. Facebook a few years ago had a market capitalization of almost $300 billion dollars with fewer than 15,000 full-time equivalent employees. Google and other high tech companies follow the same business model. A few companies worth a billion dollars have fewer than several hundred employees.

Airbnb is another ghost company with about 1000 employees, owns few rooms, but has more available rooms than the largest hotel groups in the world. By contrast, Hilton Hotels owns its rooms and has 150,000 workers. Go figure!

What should a company do? Life expectancy of the mega companies is getting shorter. For example, the life expectancy of a typical European and Japanese global company is less than 13 years. Think about it! Your employer with tens or even hundreds of thousands of Vucans may not exist in 10 years. The life expectancy of a startup or small business is less than two years.

Work Lesson Earned: In many ways, we're in ghost economy. Companies are here today, but possibly gone tomorrow. Automation, robotics, machine learning, Internet of Things, and artificial intelligence are turning all companies into tech companies. But, visceral fear is driving many management decisions:

> "The question is, how does a non-tech company become a tech company quickly? … When faced with a competitor like Amazon, do you do as Walmart did and invest heavily in tech firms and technical knowledge? Or do you go the way of Sears … into bankruptcy court?"[22]

The impacts on Vucans are profound and real. It's not fun. And, there's no going back.

AT&T - REINVENTING ITSELF & TELECOMMUNICATIONS

Change is inevitable, and the disruption it causes often brings both inconvenience and opportunity.
Robert Scoble – Technology Evangelist

"Only 8% of CEOs believe their business model will survive the current levels of large-scale digital disruption."[23] Digital disruption is the use of tech to make an organization competitive. This is only one piece of the puzzle. The competitive challenge involves changing worker's hearts and minds. Let's look at both sides of the AT&T disruption story.

AT&T has been around for over a hundred years. The CEO of AT&T wants to reinvent the company. However how do you shift a battleship or huge organization quickly? It's not easy. EVERY large company faces this:

> "Today, Randall Stephenson, AT&T's chairman chief executive, is trying to reinvent the company so it can compete more deftly. Not that long ago it had to fight for business with other phone companies and cellular carriers. Then the internet and cloud computing came along, and AT&T found itself in a tussle with a whole bunch of companies."

Digitalization involves architecting, designing, and deploying a competitive business model, tech, processes, projects, products and services:

> "By 2020, Mr. Stephenson hopes AT&T will be well into its transformation into a computing company that manages all sorts of digital things: phones, satellite television and huge volumes of data, all sorted through software managed in the cloud."

AT&T workers were hired, promoted, and reinforced for one set of behaviors and must adopt new behaviors and learn digital tech. So, how does a company convert analog hearts and minds to digital. Huge challenge.

Work Lesson Earned: The rest of the story. The Board and the CEO of AT&T have a new message for their employees. The cover of the *New York Times* article says everything: "Gearing Up for the Cloud, AT&T Tells Its Workers: 'Adapt or Else'." This is the message that is heard all over the corporate world, whether we like it or not. So, what do you think of this messaging?

KIMBERLEY-CLARK - REINVENTING ITSELF

True disruption means threatening your existing product line and your past invest-ments. Breakthrough products disrupt current lines of businesses.
Peter Diamandis – Engineer & Physician

Every organization is in the business to make money even if they are philanthro-pies. For-profit companies need to make a profit, achieve margin, and enhance their market cap for investors. Not-for-profit companies need to have sufficient monies to cover their expenses.

Every global company is trying to self-disrupt. The alternative is being disrupted by an unknown startup and going out of business. For many companies, disrup-tion fear is real and visceral. Change is part of the daily work mantra. As we've discovered, tech is doable. The Vucan part is much harder. A quick story may help:

Kimberly-Clark makes Huggies, Kleenex, and other household products. For many years, employment at Kimberly-Clark was a job for life. No more! The *Wall Street Journal* recently had an article called: 'Kimberly-Clark, Deadwood Workers Have Nowhere to Hide'. It pretty much says it all. The diaper and tissue maker is shifting its culture from a paternalistic company with life-time employ-ment to one focusing on continual improvement, efficiency, and innovation.

Kimberly-Clark uses harsh concepts to communicate competitive imperatives such 'let's get moving' and 'performance management'. So, what happens to Vucans who can't move fast enough? According to the article, Kimberly-Clark is shedding its 'dead wood workers'. Tough talk for disruptive times.

Work Lesson Earned: Legacy organizations know they're vulnerable to disrup-tion. Pressure from shareholders is oppressive. Regulators are scrutinizing every decision. Politicians rail against high executive salaries and low wages. And, organizations are going to extremes to monitor performance. Executives are on a quarterly leash to make their numbers. Performance of all workers is monitored and measured even intrusively such as monitoring individual key strokes of software coders and movement of workers.

WALMART - REINVENTING ITSELF & BIG BOX RETAIL

All organizations do change when put under sufficient pressure. This pressure must be either external to the organization or the result of very strong leadership.
Bruce Henderson - CEO Boston Consulting Group

Companies in traditional industries are the most susceptible to disruption. In our neighborhood in Portland Oregon U.S., a retailer occupies a city block. The store sells electronics, food, clothing and many items to several neighborhoods.

The store operates on thin margins and can't find Vucans to work at minimum wage. The store decided about six months ago to automate. Customers scan their own products. Store outsourced merchandising, security, and shelf stocking. This retail business model is coming much faster and sooner than many workers expected? Customers are seeing the future of retail morph in real time due to automation. Our corner retailer wants to evolve into a ghost company.

In the U.S., Walmart, Target, and Home Depot are the three largest retail employers. Walmart is famous for its enormous Supercenters, which are open 24/7 with full-time and part-time employees. However, Walmart is competing with Amazon and other online retailers. Walmart is taking a hybrid approach to remain competitive, investing in automation and its workers by offering higher wages, online training, and paid degree programs. Walmart is a people intensive business and is following the same model, but automating more slowly.

Starbucks, UPS, and many big box retailers are focusing on their workers because customers want the people experience. Employee turnover is expensive. According to surveys, turnover for each front-line worker can cost up to $5,000 or 20% to 30% of an entry-level salary. Turnover in low-wage occupations can run up to 50% in the first 6 months so there's a bottom-line inducement to retain and upskill these workers.[24]

Hard Lesson Earned: How does a non-tech company evolve into a tech company quickly and effectively? This is one of the toughest questions facing many companies. And, there's no easy answer. Since, it's based on VUCA context, segment, business model, people, systems, risk appetite, and urgency.

WEWORK - REINVENTING ITSELF & THE OFFICE

Disruption is about risk-taking. But then you become a *Fortune 500* company, which is about risk mitigation
Steve Case - Entrepreneur

We first heard about and visited a WeWork (currently We Company) office in San Francisco about seven years ago. I remember the open and glassed space where software developers were working computer-to-computer at 11:00 pm a weekend night a few days before Christmas. The developers were from all around the world. I could see that they had the startup hustle - the work addiction to build something no one else had.

We checked out WeWork shortly after. I frankly didn't get it at the time. I do now. WeWork is the Gen Z and Millennial work mecca. WeWork is the world's biggest coworking company. WeWork rents out short or long-term working space from a shared desk for creative freelancers to individual office space to larger businesses.

WeWork positions itself as a creative incubator with the right Millennial work vibe including carefully selected work colors, subdued lighting, free crafted beers, munchies, designed ambiance, and a kindred community of creatives, innovators, doers, and makers. It has 200,000 'members' in 200 class A commercial locations across 56 cities in 20 countries.

What makes WeWork business model unique? WeWork is virtual. Think Airbnb for work spaces. WeWork does not own its work space. It rents long-term. WeWork promotes a great story and work narrative. WeWork encourages the first digital generation to work in a shared location and exchange ideas. WeWork has harnessed the global zeitgeist of Millennial work.

Work Lesson Earned. In this book, we talk much about 'getting it' - understanding things at a deeper level. WeWork gets it with its Millennial and Gen Z populations. WeWork's next iteration is WeLive, which is communal and single housing for its 'members'. WeGrow is the company's elementary school "elevating the collective consciousness of the world by expanding happiness and unleashing every human's superpowers". BTW: It's valued around $47 Billion and still hasn't made a profit. So, what's next for them?

WHEN SHOULD COMPANY'S SELF-DISRUPT

All companies face 4 life-saving questions:

1. When should they self-disrupt?
2. How should they self-disrupt?
3. What's their final destination?
4. How are they going to monetize (make money)?

So, what's your company's killer new idea? All companies are searching for the next killer business model, app, platform, product, or idea. It's too late when there's simply not enough products in the pipeline to create a sustainable competitive advantage. Many companies learned this lesson the hard way. When products go stale, stagnation and revenue loss are not far behind. The auto industry learned this when it lost touch with auto buyers. Or, the wake-up call to change the existing product paradigm may come from a competitor. In the auto industry, it's now autonomous vehicles.

When the wake-up sounds to self-disrupt, it results in management and company panic. Why? Well, killer ideas can be copied quickly. Legal protection lasts only so long before someone copies or enhances an existing product or service. In information intensive companies such as consultancies, the greatest ideas can be replicated in months. So history shows: Today's hot idea is tomorrow's fad and the next day's has-been company.

For example, General Electric (GE) has had a horrible 10 years. Dozen or so years ago, it was the most valuable company in the world. It had the best management and training systems. It had the best culture of a large organization. It could do no wrong. But, **Disruption Rules**. It starting making bad business decisions based on old assumptions. It did not adapt. In the last 10 years, its market capitalization has gone down about 90% and many see the company as an also-ran. GE wants to operate as a software startup. So, how do you take a mega-company and make it into an adaptive, lean, agile, and mean startup? Good luck with that!

Work Lesson Earned: Legacy companies have internal impediments and obstacles, such static cultures, status quo thinking, dated technologies, legacy processes, and antiquated management systems. The systems have been around a long time and worked very well. These systems promoted and reinforced the status quo. In other words, its systems are not flexible and agile to respond to VUCA and disruption.

DISRUPTION IS CREATING NEW WORK WORLDS

There are lots of lessons to learn from Amazon. Never stop innovating or questioning the fundamentals of your business. Disrupt yourself before others do.
Brad Stone – Journalist & Author

Consulting firms, academics, and consultants are developing models for the *Future of Work*. Price Waterhouse Coopers (PwC) developed a scenario called the *Future of Work: A Journey to 2022*. The premise of the study is: "disruptive innovations are creating new industries and business models, and destroying old ones."[25] PwC outlined three distinct worlds of work: Blue, Green, and Orange. Let's look at each scenario because each seems plausible and may work for you.

In the Orange Work World, small is beautiful. Work is broken down into collaborative networks focused on specific projects. The driving goal for the Orange World is to maximize work flexibility, focus on lean organizations through projectizing work, and emphasize innovation to remain competitive. Orange Work World companies will be small using a just-in-time business model to produce on-demand products and deliver services. Work specialization and detailed knowledge are critical to adding personal value. Workers will have flexibility, have free time between projects, and focus on short-term contractual work.

In the Green Work World, corporate social sustainability and environmental contributions will drive organizations. Company ethical values, green thinking, sustainability, and doing the right things right are critical to adding organizational and personal value.

In the Blue Work World, business profitability, growth, margins, and market share are prominent. Global corporations compete based on innovation, resources, execution, and differentiation. Long-term job security, employability, and training are critical to workers in the Blue World. In this World, income disparity between the haves and have-nots will continue to get bigger.[26]

Work Lesson Earned: What world would you like to work in? Why? What type or types of organizations are in your current work world? How can you work for them? What are they looking for in employees? Remember, organizations in each work world still have to attract talent, plan projects, process work, reward performance, add value, and make a profit.

SELF-MANAGEMENT - YOUR NEXT STEPS

The greatest discovery of my generation is that a human being can alter his life by altering his attitude.
William James - Writer

So, you've spent valuable time reading **Working It: Disruption Rules**. Great! But, what are you going to do about it? What are your next steps?

We end each section **Working It: Disruption Rules** with a Self-Management page with critical questions. We ask these questions so you have a new lens to look at work and possibly reframe your context of **Working It**. So, we ask you, the reader, to internalize questions because self-awareness is the first step to your making smart choices about your work, career, and job:

- Do you understand the competitive and innovation pressures facing your company or client?
- Is your organization or client going through a paradigm shift or disruption? And if so, from what to what?
- Do you know what your company's Plan B or Plan C to respond to the paradigm shift?
- Do you know and can you articulate simply your organization's new work rules?
- Do you know your company's or client's digital and automation business model?
- Is the business model resilient and how does the company intend to maintain its competitive posture and maintain margin?
- How do you see these paradigm shifts impacting you?
- What do you think of the idea that it's the 'End of Business as You Know It?"
- Do you see this as securing or enhancing your value in the organization?
- Is your company outsourcing or moving work offshore?
- Is your job outsourceable?
- If you're a consultant, what value-added differentiator do you offer?
- Do you think artificial intelligence and robots will replace humans?
- Do you think that AI will replace or can replace you?
- If yes, how quickly? If no, why not?

PEOPLE

-

WORK RULES

This element of the 7P's framework deals with people or Vucans. Work is all about people. At the end of a long day, you work with people. You share ideas with people. You plan, direct, organize, and deliver with people. You innovate new products. You service people - your customers.

The Vucan or people element is probably the most difficult to address in **Working It**. Why? People don't like VUCA change. Vucans will take the path of least resistance (risk aversion).

The Vucan challenge is distilled below:

> "... people who seek a well-paying, professional track career in nearly every sector are grappling with the same challenges; reinvention of business models due to digital technology; the rise of a handful of successful 'superstar' firms; and rapidly changing understanding around loyalty and the level of mutual commitment to the employee-employer relationship."[27]

VUCAN DRIVERS - PEOPLE

Old School	New School
This too shall pass	Constant transformation here to stay
Industrial robots are static – 'pick and place', 'welding' robots	Commercial and cobots are flexible, smart, adaptive, and learning
Individual leadership	Collective leadership
MBA	Just-in-time business learning
Brick and mortar education	MOOC and online education
Fact based education	Entrepreneurial education
Fixed organizational structure	Fluid and agile organizational structure
Position based leadership	Fluid enterprise, program, project, team, and product leadership
Dream of management	Dream of startup founder, side-hustle, and freedom
CEO longevity	CEO job is short and brutal
Worker with lifelong employment	Dispensable worker based on economic conditions
Problem-solving is fixed with definitive answer	Problem-solving is risk-based with probabilities and multiple options
Thomas Edison, Peter Drucker, Alfred P. Sloan, W. Edwards Deming	Elon Musk, Jack Ma
Old work rules and expectation	New behavioral expectations
College degree meal ticket	No degree required
Reaction & fear	Respond to reaction and fear
Hiring & firing by people	Hiring & firing by bot

VUCANS @ RISK

You're either the one that creates the automation or you're getting automated.
Tom Preston-Werner - Software Developer

Robots are coming. Robots and smart machines are doing a lot of our work and will do a lot more over the next year. Take a look below:

- Machines will do 52% of worker tasks by 2025.
- Startups are re-visioning the entire food grid and food chain: food delivery services (drones), grocery stores (no people), packaging (3-D machines), and restaurants (food printing).
- Vucans can print their food at home using 3-D food printers for dry food.
- Restaurants are using 3-D printers to prepare specialized food.
- Robot can peel a head of lettuce in 27 seconds.
- Tipsy Robot bartender can make 120 cocktails per hour in Las Vegas at $12 to $16 a drink.
- Robot can assemble a simple IKEA chair in 20 minutes, while a human takes 10 to 15 minutes to assemble the same chair (if ever).
- 94.5% of doctors have the same diagnosis and treatment as a machine learning eye disease program.
- Introduction of 1 factory (industrial) robot replaces 6 workers.
- Hiring Robot can do 50,000 interviews/day for 200 client companies.
- Beijing Robotics Industry wants to produce 100,000 robots yearly by 2020.
- Da Vinci robotic surgeons have completed 50 million human surgeries.
- Universal Robots has produced 25,000 collaborative robots (cobots), which is 60% of the market.
- 50,000 Las Vegas casino workers went on strike in 2018 demanding greater job security in part from the coming automation.

Work Lesson Earned: Best case scenario, a robot is going to be your work partner and collaborator. Worst case, well … A few questions to think about: What can a robot do that you can't? What can you do that a robot can't? How will these developments impact your work/career/job? What are your work Plan B's and contingency plans? **BTW:** The above robot statistics are from various issues of 'Clocking In from MIT Technology' - a great emagazine.

VUCAN DECISION-MAKING

Lengthy reigns at the top may be the next thing to get disrupted.
Carol Ryan - *Wall Street Journal* Writer

Many CEO'S are unfit for VUCA duty. In other words, they are not 'future ready'. Take a look at what investor's say in the **Self Disruptive Leader** survey from Korn Ferry:

- "78 percent (of investors) insist the CEO is critically important when deciding in which companies to invest."
- "83 percent (of investors) cite an exceptional CEO as critical to an organization's success in disruptive times."
- **Bottom Line:** "Fewer than two in ten corporate leaders have the skills required to take their companies into the future" according to investors.[28]

A critical result of the above survey is executives can't make smart VUCA decisions quickly. In VUCA time, leadership decision-making and management problems solving seem to be lacking. Much of the same can be said of political decision-making. Got doubts? Think Brexit. Think President Trump. Think Xi Jinping.

Let's look at GE again. GE was the most valuable company 20 years ago. It had the 'best and brightest' leaders and managers. It invented much of the third industrial revolution. But, things happened. Bad adaptation. Bad leadership selection. Bad decisions. Bad timing. Much of its value has tanked along with weak profits.

The current GE CEO reported in the *Wall Street Journal* that:

> "I'm not going to put the company's reputation at further risk ... We are going to come up with guidance when we can walk people through it where the math adds up, and we can be very clear on how we are going to go about delivering on those numbers."[29]

Work Lesson Earned: So, how do executives in your organization solve problems and make decisions? How do executives manage risks? What makes them successful? So, if you're an individual contributor, would you want to be a supervisor or manager in your organization? Would you invest in your company? Why or why not?

WHO ARE VUCAN LEADERS?

You're not just trying to do something marginally, incrementally better. You're doing something that is a fundamental paradigm shift, that will have exponential impact. That means it's harder to do, but ultimately, if it's successful, the impact it has is far greater.
Steve Case - Entrepreneur

Vucan leadership: you know it when you see it. Think of people that you would consider to be Vucan leaders. I bet there's only a handful.

So, the question arises: 'What makes a Vucan leader'? This is very critical in the VUCA work world of identity politics, fake news, violence, hacking, compliance, me-too, social injustice, and many other risk issues. All of these require a new form of Vucan leadership.

Disruption may be today's crucible of Vucan leadership. Let's explain this. Vucan leadership is defined by critical circumstances. When a critical situation arises, a Vucan leader will arise. Vucan leaders are resilient risk-takers. Today, Vucan managers are rising in all areas of an organization because of competition, trade wars, corporate restructuring, information explosion, digitalization, outsourcing, automation, or simply the necessity to get the job done.

Vucan leadership is something special. When you see it, you know it. Leadership is an exemplary element of good management. Leadership is an art. Leadership is flexible and resilient depending on market requirements, organizational culture, and people's abilities. Leaders seem to manage, inspire, engage, embrace, dare, dialogue, and challenge people. Vucan leadership may integrate 'command and control' elements to 'coaching and mentoring.'

Vucan leaders have the common touch and are hands-on. Leaders are closely involved with workers, suggesting, and demonstrating as opposed to directing or managing. Leaders are self-selecting.

Leaders see an unfulfilled opportunity, need, or requirement. Nature, organizations, and the marketplace hate a vacuum. Someone will fill it. This someone is called the Vucan leader or founder. So, leadership is seen as a personal issue - a desire to monetize, commit, inspire, engage, share, and improve. This can happen on the customer service desk to the boardroom.

Work Lesson Earned: So, where have all the business and political leaders gone? Maybe, we need new definitions of leadership and new Vucan leaders to emulate. Or, may be the risk/reward of leadership no longer exists.

SO YOU WANNA BE A VUCAN MANAGER?

Management is about persuading people to do things they do not want to do, while leadership is about inspiring people to do things they never thought they could.
Steve Jobs – Apple Founder & CEO

I've always had a burning question: 'What's better, beings a Vucan leader or a manager?' I've observed first level supervisors, managers, and executives work their magic. I don't know what makes a Vucan leader or a highly effective manager. Maybe, this is moot.

Great management is a difficult topic to explain. Increasingly, leaders are seen as Vucans who can guide himself or herself or a group to do what needs to be done in a process or project. In general, these are normal Vucans who can self-manage, possess high energy, are passionate, are committed to a cause, can share responsibility, have high values, and are highly credible.

Here's a huge irony. Many Vucan leaders think of themselves as doers, makers, hands-on, etc.   When we've interviewed the direct reports of the 'leader,' we found that direct reports thought their bosses were useless administrators, control freaks, incompetent, evildoers, or information shufflers certainly not Vucan leaders or frankly not even good managers. Maybe the critical issue is not the manager or supervisory role, but the ability of a team of Vucans to work together and for individuals to self-manage.

Let's look at an orchestra conductor. Is this person a Vucan leader or manager? A great conductor as a leader takes risks, inspires, causes musicians to reach inside themselves, and creates a performance that is greater than the whole. VUCA time is also risky for musicians. It's difficult to fund and pay for an orchestra. An average conductor gets the job done and ensures that all the orchestra employees are well paid. So, I will take an imperfect performance that is inspired and passionate over an uninspired technically perfect performance.

Work Lesson Earned: The difference between a manager and Vucan leader may be noticeable. So on a personal level, ask yourself the following questions: Do you want to be a Vucan leader? Do you want to be a Vucan manager? Do you emulate good things you see in others? Do you practice personal continuous improvement? How do you deal with risks?

VUCAN EXECUTION - MAKING YOUR NUMBERS

Having finalized the 2019 budget, our focus shifts to executing our goals and hitting our marks.

CEO Nancy Dubuc says after laying off 10% of workers.[30]

I heard an executive give a talk at a conference recently. Every other word seemed to be 'execution.' It isn't good enough to come up with a killer idea or app, it has to be monetized. How? Through smart execution. This is another critical attribute of a Vucan leader.

'Making your numbers' through right execution is simply another way for saying that accountability is a critical self-management attribute. 'Do as you say and say as you do.' But, senior executives are confused as how to lead, manage, and 'make their numbers.' If they don't make their numbers, then the fear is that they too may be vulnerable and even expendable. Harsh truths of a disruptive economy and VUCA world.

This is the upside of the definition that most of us associate with 'execution'. But, there's the downside of execute, which people associate with capital punishment. The downside deals with accountability of not executing according to plan.

Making your numbers is being pushed down the organization and even into the supply chain. The risk of unintended consequences can arise. Employees trained, rewarded, and promoted for one set of behaviors, expectations, and skills are now asked or told to adopt new ones. This is very hard for many workers. And managers and bosses are also victims. For example, the common complaint is that 75% of workers don't quit their jobs, but really quit their company's new expectations and messaging.

Work Lesson Earned: Know how to execute make your numbers. For some, it's make margin or enhance market cap. For others, it's achieve cost savings. For others, it's find business opportunities (upside risks) that provide higher margins that the cost of capital. So, know your numbers, your job will depend on it whether you're a VP or a line worker.

END OF MANAGEMENT AS WE KNOW IT?

As the **Working It** title says: **Disruption Rules**. However, would you like to work for a disruptive boss, which seems to be management style adopted by many leaders and managers. Let's look at this a little closely.

"Casting oneself as a disruptive leader is in vogue these days, suggesting a bold, take-no-prisoners management style that ignites new trends and crushes competitors" says the *Wall Street Journal (WSJ)*. Work now emphasizes execution, get the job done. So, we have a new crop of disruptive leaders and managers, who want to get ahead quickly. And, this management style is adopted by wanna be Vucan leaders. And, thirty-five percent of today's college grads want to work for inspiring, go-for-it, disruptive managers.

Quick story: I've worked on and led 'death march' projects and know this. We see three types of managers: 1. Lead disruptive (risk-taking); 2. Follow (risk-sensitive); or 3. Get out of the way (risk-averse). Like a skewed bell curve, most managers are naturally #2 and #3 managers. A few or very few are natural #1's. If they are, they naturally go to a startup, sales, head a special project, or similar venture.

So, we have a lot of #2 and #3 managers, who 'fake it till they make it'. Most don't make it. For example, I've found that senior executives don't understand and can't articulate how to respond to business VUCA disruptions and paradigm shifts. They know their competitive rules and business models are different, but I'm surprised they can't articulate the changes needed to execute effectively in VUCA time. They simply don't know RBPS and don't do RBDM.

Work Lesson Earned: If the favored management model today is disruptive, how do you survive and prosper under such a boss? *WSJ* suggests:

- Cultivate an ability to pivot quickly.
- Ask your Vucan boss for help prioritizing projects to avoid overload.
- Don't take your boss's impulsive or overbearing behavior personally.
- Use your skills to complement the boss's strengths.
- Learn from the disrupter's positive traits, such as persistence.
- Know your own hot buttons to avoid reacting defensively.
- Ask colleagues for advice before offering your Vucan boss feedback.[31]

ELON MUSK – TODAY'S EDISON

A person needs to work 80-100 hours per week to change the world.
Elon Musk tweet

'Working 9 to 5 is For Losers' was the title of a recent *New York Times* article.[32] Vucans have picked up this mantra from Elon Musk, today's Thomas Edison. Elon is the hero of a generation of 'crushers', entrepreneurial startup workers.

Elon Musk serves as CEO for four companies, including Tesla, Space X, and Boring. You can see interesting Muskian work developments in **Working It**. One **Working It** shifting paradigm from Elon Musk is to pull all-nighters in his factories, where talk of 120 hour work weeks is a badge of honor. For example, his Tesla employees worked 100 hours per week at times as they increased production of the company's Tesla Model 3 sedan.[33]

Why is Elon Musk a hero to super achievers? He's a crusher. He's a dreamer. He's a doer. He's a maker. He's launching rockets. He's built a new auto company called Tesla. Is that all? He wants to colonize Mars.

The downside is there's a backlash to super achievement. Elon Musk cautions the pain tied to working those long hours 'increases exponentially'. Then on the other hand, there are Vucans who write about work-life balance because additional hours lead to crazy work, anxiety, pain, and even death.

The distance between risk-taking dreamers, doers, makers, creatives, and founders and risk-averse Vucans has become more pronounced. Each is forming work and political tribes that resent each other.

Work discussions are visceral. In the *Future of Work*, you'll hear talk of the breakup of tech, professional unions, $15 minimum wage, 30 hour work weeks, universal basic income (UBI), socialism, resistance, social justice, and end of privilege. This is happening world-wide.

Work Lesson Earned: So, he's a god to many who believe that dreams are possible and doable even if they mean going to the ends of earth, the moon, and even Mars. Elon epitomizes manifest space destiny for humankind.

VIRTUAL VUCANS

"... computers are now doing many things that used to be the domain of people only. The pace and scale of this encroachment into human skills is relatively recent and has profound economic implications. Perhaps the most important of these is that while digital progress grows the overall economic pie, it can do so while leaving some people, or even a lot of them, worse off."[34]
Erik Brynjolfsson and Andy McAfee – Authors of Race Against the Machine

Would you like to see your favorite actor in a movie, TV program, or Netflix? Or, would a computer generated facsimile of a similar actor work just as well for you? Or, at what point is the quality and illusion of reality good enough?

Acting and modeling jobs will be impacted by computer generated imagery and robotics. Hollywood production companies consider the cost of 'world class' actors to be prohibitively expensive not to mention dealing with prima donna behaviors. As well, world renown models are no longer mannequins simply walking down the fashion runway. Models are global personalities and influencers. And, they're expensive. So, what to do?

Why not replace actors entirely with computer generated facsimiles? Just think about it? Producers and directors already are using computer generated imagery and avatars in place of actors. In a few years, advanced avatars will replace actors and models as holograms look human and their voices have emotional resonance.

At the same time, avatar models will walk down fashion runways. The observers on the side of the runway will be virtual participants viewing the show through virtual and augmented reality headsets.

Work Lesson Earned: Movies and TV are harbingers of things about to happen at work. Some believe the future of robotics may be humanoid assemblies of us or even of pets. The future is not that far away as automation and robotics point to coming paradigm shifts.

PROFESSIONAL DISRUPTION – NEXT BIG, BIG THING

People change when they hurt enough that they have to change, learn enough that they want to change, receive enough that they are able to change.
John C. Maxwell - Author

Professionals are being disrupted. Not too many years before the internet, journalists, lawyers, engineers, and doctors were paid large salaries due to their privileged information and special knowledge. These professionals had spent many years in school acquiring special knowledge and the ability to apply it for professional problem-solving and decision-making in their discrete domains.

Then the internet happened. The internet made all this professional data and information available on the web for anyone around the world to access at no cost. So what's the role of these professionals when every smart phone is connected to the internet. Professionals will have to innovate and develop personal brands to differentiate their abilities and offerings.

As content is commoditized, professionals will have to apply the content in terms of smart problem-solving and decision-making. These skills are not taught in school where regurgitation of interesting facts is the basis of most education:

> "And computers (hardware, software, and networks) are only going to get more powerful and capable in the future, and have an ever-bigger impact on jobs, skills, and the economy. ... Our technologies are racing ahead but many of our skills and organizations are lagging behind. So it's urgent that we understand these phenomena, discuss their implications, and come up with strategies that allow human workers to race ahead with machines instead of racing against them".[35]

Work Lesson Earned: Professionals are disrupted and disillusionment is setting in among lawyers, doctors, journalists, and engineers. They're thinking it's better being the disruptor than being the disruptee. When a famous perp was asked why does he rob banks, the robber said: 'That's where the money is'. Doctors want to be engineers. Lawyers want to work in tech. That's what's happening in tech. Professionals want to make the move to tech because there's a universal perception that all work is disrupted and tech is where opportunities and the money are.

CLERICAL MEDICAL VUCANS

How Tech Can Turn Doctors into Clerical Workers
Title of *New York Times* Article

I bounced the above article among several of my doc buddies. The conversation went like: "You spent 10 years going to med school. Now, you push paper. And, BTW: you may be replaced by a robot." "Huh. Yeah. Well. …."

Not good for one of the most respected professions. But, an undisputable sign of concern among one of the most lucrative and immensely respected professions. It's all about medical disruption. Medical learning machines can assess, diagnose and even predict increasingly better than medical professionals. AI can predict cancers. AI can diagnose skin cancer better than dermatologists. AI can predict seizures better than neurologists. In the near future the machine will be able to look at many health markers and predict a person's lifespan with 95% certainty. [36]

If MD's are highly pedigreed clerical workers, one physician asked: "It's enough to make doctors like myself wonder why we spent a decade in medical training learning the art of diagnosis and treatment."[37]

Patients are also getting smarter. Patients are quickly learning that they can get a virtual diagnosis relatively cheaply and quickly through the web. Think about when you went to a doctor what did you do? Probably, you went to WebMD to check out your symptoms and see what you've probably got. Then, you go to the doctor to get a real diagnosis and second opinion.

Docs are asking the same question: 'what do prospective doctors want to be when they grow up'? There was an interesting article in LinkedIn about how tech is attracting young doctors. The numbers are stunning. For example, 47% of young doctors and pharmacists are interested in moving to tech. Why? These early career risk-takers are lured by the vision of meaningful and substantive work at lot higher pay. They're told that med schools, business schools, and traditional companies are no longer the highest meal ticket and the best problem for hustle-oriented Vucans.[38]

Work Lesson Earned: So, what's the future of medicine and doctors? They will provide patients with a second opinion after a machine algorithm diagnosis. The docs will review the algorithm's assessment, diagnosis, and ethical biases. They may provide the human touch of patient communications, intuition, judgment, understanding, and empathy.

UNEMPLOYED LEGAL VUCANS

The basic premises of how the economy works have shifted under our feet and the government will have to respond.
Gautam Mukunda - Writer

Can you imagine a medical or legal conversation with Alexa? You're not far away from smart machine medical and legal assistance.

Another career impacted by automation is the legal profession. Machines can conduct legal research and background work more efficiently and economically than an army of $500 an hour lawyers.

Legal automation already does e-discovery. A machine can search, curate, interpret, and analyze legal documents involved in a lawsuit much faster and cheaper the lawyers. The machine can extract and analyze relative information that is used in millions of documents just as accurately and capably as lawyers.

This is the reason why law schools are seeing diminished attendance. Law school applications are heading south each year reflecting fewer work opportunities, soaring tuition, crushing student debt, and legal automation. Law schools are calling the above disruption a:

> "revolution in law with the time bomb on their admissions book. ... Thirty years ago if you were looking to get on the escalator to upward mobility, you went to business or law school. Today, the law school escalator is broken."[39]

Work Lesson Earned: The obituary for many professions may go like this:

> "It seems likely that the top 10 to 20 percent of any profession — be they computer programmers, civil engineers, musicians, athletes or artists — will continue to do well," he told me. "What happens to the bottom 20 percent or even 80 percent, if that is the delineation? Will the bottom 80 percent be able to compete effectively against computer systems that are superior to human intelligence?"[40]

REDUNDANT VUCAN PROFESSORS

You're not special!
Essence of Commencement Address

Each college and university has 10 or more professors teaching the same class, such as Marketing 101 or Economics 101. Most instructors have the same knowledge, skills, and abilities in their respective disciplines.

So, what is the value-added differentiator in an educator or a college? College or instructor branding? May be! Some colleges are ivy-league branded. Some professors may be more inspirational, have more wisdom, have more pedigree, and be more engaging instructors than others.

But, many introductory classes have 200 to 500 students in a huge auditorium. Real instruction is conducted by teaching assistants, who have their own priorities. There are lots of instructors on YouTube who offer the same information for free. And if you want to be self-taught, there are hundreds of free resources on the web.

Multiply this situation by 1000's of universities in one country with the same Marketing and Economics classes. Sounds like a market ripe for disruption, disintermediation, and friction reduction through just-in-time and online education.

One or even 2 professors in a discipline may be laureates, world-class, and exceptional instructors. If they're entrepreneurial, they can develop marketing curriculum and educate thousands using the internet. This may be the future of education as many professors impart the same information. So, it seems with sky high costs in the U.S. and many countries, education is ripe for disruption.

Work Lesson Earned: So, back to the key question: What is the value-added differentiator in a college or professor? This is a critical question and a huge issue for education the world over.

Ask the same questions about your specific knowledge domain, qualifications, credentials, functions, etc.

DIGITAL MEDIA VUCANS

Everything you thought you knew about the workplace is already outdated.
Fast Company Magazine

Just a year ago, digital media, content branding, media curation, online product creation, and online journalism were among the hottest and employable professions. Content was king (OK queen).

Every company needed a strong online presence. Millennial Vucans wanted honest news not fakery. Millennials had discretionary incomes with profitable side-hustles. Gen Z, the first true digital generation, wanted engagement and authenticity. Traditional marketing was moving online and was the biggest platform for advertising even bigger than TV. Facebook, Snapchat, Instagram, and Twitter were media mega ballers. The online marketing vectors pointed in the right direction.

All media was pumped on the possibilities and even probabilities for a bright future and huge paydays. Bold entrepreneurial innovators, risk-takers, and VC's invested in the digital media future. But like similar tribes and Vucans, they believed their own BS echo-chamber. Well things got disrupted. BuzzFeed, Huffington Post, TechCrunch, Verizon, and Yahoo downsized thousands of digital media professionals. Buzzfeed fired 15% of its workers who two years ago thought that any digital media meant guaranteed work. Digital media professionals bemoan:

> "Working in digital media is like trying to build a fort out of marshmallows on a foundation made of marbles in a country ruled by capricious and tyrannical warring robots."[41]

It's now all about 'show me the money'? This is the key mantra of companies formed from the mega-tech companies, startups, and struggling corner retailer.

Work Lesson Earned: So, would you recommend digital media to your kids?

> "I've toiled in this business for nearly 20 years, and even in the best of times it has been a squeamish and skittering ride, the sort of career you'd counsel your kids to avoid in favor of something less volatile and more enduring — bitcoin mining, perhaps."[42]

BTW: Bitcoin is among the most speculative ventures around.

WORK FUTURES

To thrive, all businesses must focus on the art of self-disruption. Rather than wait for the competition to steal your business, every founder and employee needs to be willing to cannibalize their existing revenue streams in order to create new ones. All disruption starts with introspection.

Jay Samit - Investor & Entrepreneur

Years ago, I was running a project. The project was over budget and over schedule. Not good! I did a lessons learned on the project, when it was done. A lessons learned is a post mortem of project risks – what went right, what went wrong, and what could be improved. One Vucan on my project team compared me to one of those Dilbert clueless managers. The irony was I'd thought I'd done a pretty good job.

So, I wondered what made a good manager and where did management come from. A few years ago, I did a little research to understand the background of management. Management was invented in the 19th century. The root of the word 'management' comes from the Latin manus, meaning 'hand,' 'power,' or 'jurisdiction. Interesting! It fits. And In the medieval English contract, property stewards administered large landed estates and were required to deliver receipts or revenues 'by hand' to the property owner. The stewards were required to know every element of the business under their control. In England, the term 'manager' was adopted widely around the 16th Century and is even referenced in Shakespeare's plays.

It's surprising that it hasn't matured much in the age of digitization and an era where Asia is ascendant. Vucan requirements focus on identity, fairness, and justice. New business models have developed. Tech has accelerated. Automation robotics are implemented daily. However, management in many ways is mired in the 20th century.

Hard Lesson Earned: So if you're a manager, employee, or itinerant professional, what does management mean to you? Do you want to move into management?

WE'RE ALL TECH VUCANS

Training and development consistently emerges as one of the areas employees are least satisfied with, and lack of opportunity for growth and advancement is second only to low pay as a source of work stress.
O'Reilly Next Economy News

Organizations must think and execute like a startup? But, behavioral change is hugely challenging. And, how are they inducing employees to learn tech and act like founders as the following indicates:

> "Understanding technology is becoming an expectation in all roles within the workforce and as the workplace continues to evolve, everyone needs the critical thinking and problem-solving skills that STEM (Science, Technology, Engineering, Math) education fosters"[43]

Tech workers are in huge demand. Tech workers can be engineering and STEM college graduates. Tech workers can be self-learned. Self-learning through just-in-time courses is great for Vucans that can code, design, make, and execute, all of which add and create value for the organization.

Currently in the U.S., there are 6 million unfilled jobs for techies. And, this is the situation in many parts of the world. There are insufficient Vucans who want and can do these tech jobs.

Companies are recruiting engineering and tech talent in high school. This mirrors what is routine in sports or colleges that want competitive teams to enhance the visibility and marketability of the school. And, companies are not requiring formal engineering or tech degrees but will pay high wages for high-school students who can immediately add value to the organization.[44]

Work Lessons Earned: If we're all gonna be tech workers, we're in trouble. A lot of folks didn't pass basic math, much less coding. What are they gonna do?

ITINERANT VUCANS

A career is a job you love, right? That's what a career should be. If you're in a job that you hate, you should quit. That's the way I look at it. I'm in a job that I love, so I'm going to make it my career.
Cameron Sinclair – Designer & Humanitarian

The lifelong project career path is evolving inside and outside organizations. You may be a professional, specialist, or craftsperson. What characterizes you is your portable and marketable skills. You're becoming an itinerant professional. A software engineer learns new software languages and goes where the market is. A lawyer with special skills, such as environmental law, works virtually on litigation cases.

Can you see a CEO as an itinerant professional? Well guess what? CEO's are taking their bags and moving from company to company. Why? They go to where they're needed as CEO's become itinerant professionals, they hopscotch across industry boundaries. A banker may run an electric utility and vice versa. According to studies, a third of the CEOs parachute in from outside the company. What do these portable CEOs have in common? They may not know the guts of the product but they have the skills, grit, and guts to make (manage) work decisions and transform (lead) an organization. In other words, they have the right Vucan management and leadership stuff.

Another interesting trend is that career satisfaction and success for will depend on developing core competencies and then displaying them in projects. These projects preferably are on your customer's or employer's critical growth and profit path.

Work Lesson Earned: Pay attention to getting cross-industry and cross-functional experience. The career, work, and job disruptors described in this book are real. They're not going away. All Vucans will be impacted.

WHATCHA GONNA DO?

Welcome to a working world that doesn't understand you, might not want to hire you, and definitely doesn't want to pay you very much.
Fortune Magazine

Underemployed. Unemployed. Angry. Resentful. Nowhere to go.

This seems to be the story of many of Millennials and Gen Z'ers throughout the world who are unemployed or underemployed. By the way, this is a global phenomenon. Look at Uganda, Hong Kong, and U.S. riots.

There are more college graduates than high paying jobs. This is caused much angst in many family households in the U.S. and throughout the world. The numbers are discouraging:

> "Fully 20% of men aged 24 to 55 did not have full-time jobs and nearly half of all new college graduates are unable to find a job that comports with their education."[45]

Every week, we talk with parents whose children cannot find gainful employment. The parents are very successful lawyers, engineers, or physicians. They seem embarrassed over their kids, who were the 'best and brightest' in high school and went to the best colleges. However, they got non-marketable college degrees in Russian film, gender studies, French art history, or similar topic.[46]

These parents are privileged through hard work. They usually co-signed or picked up all the college loans. Many parents feel that branded college and university was the means for their children to find themselves emotionally and occupationally. The unsaid is that it was an awfully expensive experiment that may have diminished ROI and not meet expectations as the following indicates:

> "A recent survey conducted by the Pew Research Centre showed that a mere 16% of Americans think that a four-year degree course prepares students very well for a high paying job in the modern economy.[47]

Work Lesson Earned: Along with the impacts of automation, there's simply not enough high paying work to go around in a tech-driven, globalized economy. Graduates simply do not have the life, work, and tech skills to work and understand disruption rules.

UNPREPARED GRADUATING VUCANS

Gartner says only 20 percent of employees have the skills needed for both their current role and their future career.

Gartner - Consulting Organization

Millennials around the world may be a lost work generation'. One major reason is most recent college graduates are not prepared for work through poor self-management. The numbers are stunning:

> "While 96% of chief academic officers of colleges and universities believe that their institutions are very or somewhat effective at preparing students for the workforce, only 11% of business leaders strongly agree."[48]

The table below reveals the **Employer** (top bar) vs. **Student** (bottom bar) perceptions of work competencies[49]. It seems that students are not work-ready.

Employer vs. Student Perception of Work Competencies

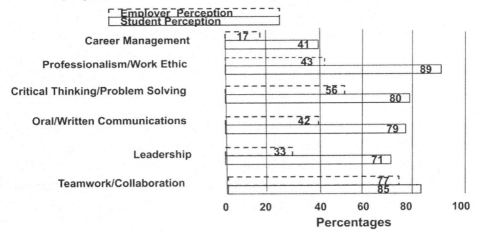

Work Lesson Earned: The above table shows graduates are not work- ready and are under employed or unemployed. Graduates will have to readjust their beliefs, thoughts, and behaviors regarding career management, work ethics, communications, and self-management.

"I KIND OF RUINED MY LIFE BY GOING TO COLLEGE"

The above title was from a *Consumer Reports Magazine* cover article. Lots of articles on this. 'Most Americans with Student Debt Regret it?' is a similar story in *Motley's Fool Magazine.*[50] The bad news is college remorse: nearly 75% (college students) wish they'd made different decisions' about college and loans.

I keep coming back to this theme throughout the book. College Vucans and their parents are mired in old paradigms, believing any college degree will pay for itself even though there is little marketability for it.

The risk/return value of a college education is questionable. The hurricane of creative destruction is overwhelming higher education. In the U.S., the cost of college education has risen much faster than earnings. Currently, there's a huge debate on the value of a college degree in terms of personal investment in time and money. Or simply, is college an experience to find yourself worth it?

"Specifically, for business and other liberal-arts majors, the prestige of the school has a major impact on future earnings expectations. But for fields like science, tech, engineering and math, it largely doesn't matter whether students go to a prestigious, expensive school or a low-priced one—expected earnings turn out the same" says *New York Times.*[51]

Another discussion is the value of an elite college degree always leading to employability and higher salaries regardless of the degree. A study was conducted analyzing thousands of college graduates and their salaries 10 years after graduation. The *Wall Street Journal* reported:

> "Diplomas from prestigious schools boost future earnings only in certain fields, while in other fields they simply don't make a difference."[52]

Work Lesson Earned: College is an investment. College has a Return on Investment (ROI). If your family is mega privileged, (1 percenters) then live the dream and spend lavishly to find yourself in college. For the rest of us, the other 99%, get real with yourself and your family. Otherwise, you're in for a life of indentured servitude to college loans.

NO COLLEGE DEGREE - NO PROBLEM

What's your value-add to me – your employer? This is what most employers think? Tough thinking. Well, that's the basis of a free market economy.

My doc's brother went to Harvard and got a history degree. The world doesn't employ too many historians. What to do? Later in life the Harvard grad reinvented himself as an elite coder. The problem is he makes as much money as a community college trained coder in the same company. What do these Vucans have in common? They can do the same value-adding task (coding) pretty much the same way. They're also quick and adaptable lifelong learners.

Many companies in 2019 announced they will stop requiring college degrees. Tim Cook, Apple CEO, said that half of Apple's workers did not have a 4-year college degree.[53] These companies evaluate a person's capabilities through online or on-site testing. Why? They found "there's little or no correlation between success at university and success in careers."[54]

Over the last 6 years, there have been weekly articles on the value of college, specifically of a liberal arts degree. College is very expensive in the West. The cost of a college education indentures parents and the student with unforgiveable loans paying for the unmarketable degree over many years. Millennial results are pretty known. Millennials are delaying families, not purchasing a home, and are even living with their parents into their mid-30s.

This comes down to a lack of RBPS and RBDM by college graduates and their parents. Parents co-signed their kid's loans out of filial respect, extended parenting, not understanding the ROI of a particular degree, lifetime salary earnings, skills training, requirements of the student loan debt, graduate employability, and *Future of Work*.

Work Lesson Earned: So, do you need a prestige college pedigree to demonstrate your value? Value can be knowledge, wisdom, abilities, skills, and other marketable attributes. The irony is employers are saying: 'no college degree - no problem'.

ONCE YOU THINK YOU 'GOT IT', THEN ...

We don't see things as they are, we see them as we are.
Anais Nin - Author

The planet is shifting into an epochal change. Climate change seems to be the beginning of a global paradigm shift – something the earth hasn't seen in thousands of years. But facing any significant change, there are deniers – good Vucans that don't 'get it'.

Several years ago, there was an ad for Putnam Investments: "You think you understand the situation, but what you don't understand is that the situation just changed." Amen! When I think I've just got it, 'got' and 'it' both seem to change. This is on a global, business, and personal level. And, it's scary! I don't like the sudden change.

Disruption and change are inherent in all paradigm shifts. Disruption distorts our perceptions of our life and work. Disruption can distort our reality - the 'is' of what is happening around us.

If you believe VUCA, disruption,, and risks are the new normal, then a critical issue is how will businesses and Vucans cope, sustain, and compete in VUCA time. This will be a critical issue for all Vucans.

Disruption is distressing. You then react according to your false perceptions of the 'is', which if distorted by old career assumptions or work rules and how you respond to your work, career, and job. This results in a vicious cycle.

Work Lesson Earned: George Bernard Shaw, the philosopher, offers wisdom. He said that the world is populated by three kinds of Vucans: 1. Those who make things happen; 2. Those to whom it happens; and 3. Those who wonder what happened?

If there's one thing I want you to walk away from **Working It: Disruption Rules** is that it's much better to be clued in rather than clueless. And, I want you to be in the first Shaw category: 1. Those who make things happen. Or in other words, you want to be a disruptor, NOT a disruptee.

KNOW YOUR CAREER KILLERS: YOUR FUTURE DEPENDS ON IT!

People don't change their behavior unless it makes a difference for them to do so.
Sharon Stone - Actor

I know lots of tech wizards in software, finance, and engineering. These wizards are uber geeks and they rule! Only one problem! Many wizards are turkeys with people. They lack people or social skills. These nice Vucans went into tech thinking they could solve problems, make the world a better place, or simply to make a lot money. They're all OK.

These are capable Vucans and good professionals. However, they reached a social ceiling in their work and career. Much like the glass ceiling that thwarted women's career progression, the social ceiling is the inability for socially challenged and inarticulate professionals to progress in their careers, work, or jobs.

Probably, one-quarter to one-half of executives and many engineers are in deep trouble due to poor people, poor nuancing, and poor communication skills. Engineer founders and techies are getting to the top of the food chain. They have replaced Wall Street equity managers as the new 1% evil-doers.

Techies are great at coding and designing. However, the current business climate is forcing executives and engineers to provide testimony or communicate business plans. And, it's pathetic. Most techies are inarticulate, reactive, and oblivious of what to say. Think me-too challenged. At any organizational level, an immature outburst, harassment, or project team rebellion will put a career in jeopardy. These are career killers. And quite frankly, they don't care.

There are lots of examples of this. Physicians don't communicate well with patients or as commonly heard, the doc's bedside manner could be improved. Accountants (CPAs) in Big 4 firms rise up the technical track to become partners, but can't handle the people side or the selling side. Lawyers, who make partner through great litigation, but can't shake the money tree to get new clients. Engineer founders, who are so introverted and introspective, can't work as part of the development team. All of these are career killers.

Work Lesson Earned: Read Marshall Goldsmith's book **What Got You Here - Won't Get You There**. The bottom line is your professional skills that got you to your present level of success probably won't get you to the next level. Look at our next story to check Goldsmith's career killers.

WHAT GOT YOU HERE – WON'T GET YOU THERE!

Change is the law of life. And those who look only to the past or present are certain to miss the future.
John F. Kennedy – President of the U.S.

I like books that 'tell it like it is.' No sugar coating risks and bad behaviors. Marshall Goldsmith – the consummate executive coach – came up with the 20 self-management habits that will stop you from getting here to there:

- **Habit #1:** Winning too much.
- **Habit #2:** Adding too much value.
- **Habit #3:** Passing judgment.
- **Habit #4:** Making destructive comments.
- **Habit #5:** Starting with 'No,' 'But,' or 'However.'
- **Habit #6:** Telling the world how smart you are.
- **Habit #7:** Speaking when angry.
- **Habit #8:** Negativity, or 'Let me explain why that won't work.'
- **Habit #9:** Withholding information.
- **Habit #10:** Failing to give proper recognition.
- **Habit #11:** Claiming credit that you don't deserve.
- **Habit #12:** Making excuses.
- **Habit #13:** Clinging to the past.
- **Habit #14:** Playing favorites.
- **Habit #15:** Refusing to express regret.
- **Habit #16:** Not listening.
- **Habit #17:** Failing to express gratitude.
- **Habit #18:** Punishing the messenger.
- **Habit #19:** Passing the buck.
- **Habit #20:** An excessive need to be me.

Work Lesson Earned: Great list, but a little dated. A few things are missing from the list: No me-too sensitivity! Lack of personal hygiene. Bad habits. Life-long learning on your own nickel. Sex with subordinates. Regardless, buy, read, underline, and apply **What Got You Here - Won't Get You There**. Then, ask your best friend and may be harshest critic – your significant other - to rate you on each of the above habits. It'll be eye opening! There're lots of personal lessons learned. Have I done it with my wife? Yes. Did I like it? No!

DO YOU HAVE THE RIGHT STUFF?

Be the best at what you do or the only one doing it.
Jay Samit – Manager, Writer & Entrepreneur

Many fresh MBAs want to go into management thinking that's the way to power, perks, and bucks. I don't want to seem like a Cassandra, but …. There are lots of disruptions occurring in management. This is great if you've got the emotional maturity and 'right stuff'.

A new ailment is running through organizations: management phobia. Many Vucans don't want to be managers and existing managers want to jump off the track. The reasons vary: 'I want freedom', 'I don't want to attend so many #@% meetings!', 'I want a life', 'This is Bullsh*t', 'I want time with my kids', I have 30 nits working for me', or 'I don't want the pressure'. So, Vucans are saying 'no' to the promotion or to the move.

Management is much tougher than it was even 5 years ago due to globalization, disruption, outsourcing, off shoring, flat growth, pressures on cost margins, me-too, regulations, and possible recession. In addition, management authority has diminished. Salary compression results in fewer financial benefits for the professional manager?

Another challenge: a founder of a startup may be an asocial engineer – great with tech and lousy with people. The VC firm may hire a professional CEO, who has been there and done that to ensure IPO success. You can find new management arrangements such as co-presidents, outsourced CEO, founders and sole practitioner leaders.

What's going on? Techies, engineers, coders, and creatives don't want the headaches of compliance, people, identities, and legal wrangling. They can get all the money they want through an IPO without the accompanying organizational headaches. The founder says: 'Who cares'? I'll stay around until I get my shares, go public, and say sayonara. In the meantime, I'll play around with tech. This is all too common as engineers develop new apps, IP, and products and flip their companies.

Work Lesson Earned: There are other **Working It** ways, including being a highly paid individual contributor, influencer, maker, maven, or founder. What work do you want to do? Do you have the right stuff to be a good manager? Do you want or are you aware of the sacrifices you may have to make? And, is this the right track for you?

VUCAN WORK METAPHOR

I'm going to have a project-based life rather than a job-based life.
David Plotz – Journalist

Work metaphors offer visuals, beacons, insights scripts, and lessons. Metaphors provide us a vision of what to expect from work. The career ladder is a great visual metaphor. A person started at the bottom and with the right effort climbed each rung. The career ladder told us what the organization, its work, and expectations were for each of us.

The career ladder is pretty much dead. A career follows a zig-zag journey of knowledge acquisition and personal fulfillment. However, the ladder metaphor was inspirational because it implied there was always an opportunity for a promotion and a place to go.

One commonly heard metaphor is you're becoming an actor in the theater of work. A Vucan will move from job to job, project to project much like actors move from play to play, production to production on TV, radio, movies, and Broadway. Some roles are starring - most are supporting.

Or, your career moves are described in terms of horizontal or lateral progression in a webbed organization. You start at the middle and move outwards on one of the strands. Sometimes, you detour on a lateral strand to start a new career, job, or even a business. This is happening with Vucans doing startups.
Or, is your career a patchwork quilt? You develop value-adding skills and move around a chessboard or patchwork quilt. While these metaphors are not as powerful and inspirational as the career ladder, one will arise that most of us will accept.

Work Lesson Earned: We all have a vision or script how our work-life will enfold. It's standard with all of us. We go to college. We learn about ourselves. We get a degree. We then get married, buy a house and have 2 ½ kids. In VUCA time in a VUCA world, this scenario can change abruptly due to off-screen risk events. Our optimistic world view based on new work paradigms are shifting our expectations. Adaptability and resilience then become a work necessity. So, what's your work and career metaphor? BTW: There is no right answer. Just an important fact of work that you need to think about.

NO MORE HOMESTEADING

Most powerful question leader can ask: 'How can I help you do your job better'?

John Baldoni - Writer/author

Line workers have been treated like LIFO inventory – **L**ast **I**n – **F**irst **O**ut. But executives making millions a year are in the 'execution' bucket. Do. Do good. Meet targets. No quarterly numbers. No job.

Not too many years ago, I knew executives, who thought they could homestead a job until retirement. The executives felt they were privileged and entitled. They went to the right schools. They had significant career successes. They had steady promotions throughout their careers. If he/she didn't make their numbers, no problemo. There was always next quarter.

VUCA has disrupted executive rules of work. It became important for this Vucan to execute – in other words make his or her numbers. The company expected and required adherence to new policies of behavior for executives. Breach me-too behavioral rules - you're out. Don't make your numbers - you're out.

Let's look at Apple as it attempts to disrupt itself. The *Wall Street Journal* reported that it "is shaking up leadership and reordering priorities across its services, artificial intelligence, hardware, and retail divisions as it works to reduce the company's reliance on iPhone sales."[55] What does this mean: "high profile hires, noteworthy departures, meaningful promotions, and consequential restructurings." [56] Part of the new normal.

What's interesting is that directors and second level managers are given the mandate to make their objectives or suffer similar consequences as the execs. With increasing VUCA, companies are cutting non-performers. And, this is now cascading? A few years ago, it was the senior executive, who had the cold sweats in the middle of the night wondering if he or she was the next person to be rightsized. Managers are sweating to meet compliance (no subordinate dating), revenue, sales and other performance objectives.

Work Lesson Earned: Ask yourself the following: Do you know what numbers your boss and your boss's boss have to make? Do you know their plans on making their numbers? How does your boss rate your work to his or her value contribution? What are your numbers? Are you making them?

POWER OF SELF-MANAGEMENT

If you don't design your own life plan, chances are you'll fall into someone else's plan. And guess what they have planned for you? Not much.

Jim Rohn – Author and Entrepreneur

Self-management is the art of taking responsibility and the science of taking control of your behavior, health, spirit, work, career, and life. Think of self-management as the way to have options, make smart choices, and ultimately be free. So, think about these key self-management questions:

- What are your strengths?
- What are your values?
- Where do you belong?
- How do you work and perform?
- What value can and do you contribute?[57]

Peter Drucker, the father of management, posed these questions 15 years ago. They have particular resonance for Vucans. Many Vucans are simply not equipped, ready, or resilient to deal with disruption. The numbers are depressing. About 75% of Vucan are anxious, depressed, and have insomnia. While these are U.K. and U.S. numbers, you can see the same in many countries.

Self-management is a common theme woven through this book. Your answers to the above questions can be an early indicator of how well you're doing to understand, control, and adapt to disruption and automation coming to your life and work. We call this your self-management index. The higher your index, the better you'll manage risks and solve critical problems in your life.

Work Lesson Earned: Think your boss or your company is going to look out for you? Think again. You're entering the do-it-yourself (DIY) world of work and career management age. Companies don't offer much guidance. Vucan life and work is all about self-awareness and self-management. We believe these practices are the basis for success. Think about it. If most professional data and information are accessible on the web, what is your personal value differentiator?

SELF-MANAGEMENT – YOUR NEXT STEPS

Knowing when and how to self-disrupt are among the key self-management questions that you need to ask. Take a look at the below questions:

- Do you know who are the Vucan leaders and role models in your organization?
- What makes them effective and efficient? Or not?
- Do your Vucan managers know the present game (competitive) rules? And, do they communicate them to you?
- Do you want to go into management?
- Do you know the rules (wants, needs and expectations) of the management game in your organization?
- Where would you like to be and what do you have to do to get there?
- What do you need to do to get from 'here to there'?
- What are your numbers and what do you do to make them?
- What work rules have changed for you?
- What's your career metaphor (i.e. ladder, web, etc.)?
- Do you have a career roadmap?
- What's important to you about work?
- What's your compelling story?
- Are you secure with your work/career/job?
- Where would you like to be with your work/career/job?
- Are you a risk-taker or risk-averse?
- Are you happy with your work, career, or job?
- And if not, what are you going to do about it?
- What are you good at?
- What do you compete on?
- What is your value differentiator?
- What is your unique selling proposition?
- What's happening in your profession?
- What will people pay for that you do well?
- Do you want to be a Vucan manager?

- What leadership abilities do you have or want to have?
- Can you change workplace roles, as a Vucan manager, leader or coach?
- What makes you change roles?
- Do you react or respond to disruption?
- What's your value proposition at work?
- What do you think could be your 'value proposition'?
- How do you know it's valuable to your employer or customer?

PRINCIPLES

-

FINDING YOUR

TRUE NORTH

Principles part of the 7P's framework is based on finding and discovering your 'why' of work. Simon Sinek in **Start With Why** suggests you should understand your 'why' of work before you commit yourself to an employer, side-hustle, or startup.

Answering the 'why' defines the purpose or principle of work so you can live and work authentically. So, ask yourself the following questions:

- What's your dream career, job, or work?
- Why are you doing what you're doing?
- Why are you working for your current employer?
- More why's?

For example, work is a calling for many workers called 'workism' or the 'Gospel of Work'. What do you think of the following:

The Challenge:

"For the college-educated elite, work has morphed into a religious iden-tity—promising identity, transcendence, and community, but failing to deliver."

The Response:

"It is the belief that work is not only necessary to economic production, but also the centerpiece of one's identity and life's purpose".[58]

VUCAN DRIVERS – PRINCIPLES

Old School	New School
This too shall pass	Transformation is here to stay
No or little meaning at work	Work has meaning and purpose
No personal direction	Discover your true north
Anxiety and fear	Vucans practicing mindfulness
Work as a meal ticket	Work as a calling and gospel
'Get it' is not important	'Getting it' is situational awareness and context
Epidemic of anxiety and panic	Search for life and work happiness
No flow zone	Flow zone
Get by	Do the right things
Reaction	Response
No care	Self-care
Management of and by others	Self-management
Freudenschade	Joy in other's successes
FOMO (Fear of Missing Out)	JOMO (Joy Of Missing Out)
Freudenschade	Happiness for others
IQ	Adaptability/Sustainability Quotient
Favoritism	Performance (Execution)
Brains & privilege & pedigree	Performance (Execution)
Evaluation bias	People performance analytics
Implied comments	Radical candor
Homestead	Rise and grind

PRINCIPLES @ RISK

Work is one way people share experiences, become part of a community, and feel fulfilled and purposeful.
David Schmittlein - MIT School of Management

Walk around the cubes at work and look closely at what Vucans have on their desks, pictures of loved ones and maybe a religious symbol. Is this the latest fad at work or is a lasting phenomenon? Well, it's estimated that 80% of employees engage in workplace contemplation or spiritual practice.

Finding meaning at work can mean different things to Vucans such as supporting corporate social responsibility, working on global warming, giving back, supporting family leave, fighting for social justice, improving society, or saving the world.

Finding meaning at work is much like finding a calling in life such as being a chaplain or nurse. Finding meaning, spirit, and the soul of the workplace is not pure altruism. It's often a reaction to toxic workplaces, lack of social justice, lack of job security, changing employer-employee contract, and unmet expectations. Many want more out of work than a paycheck.

So how does meaningful work start? Meaningful work emerges from the relationship you have with the work you do. If you go to work just to make money, chances are that you'll reach saturation point relatively quickly and then you'll need to find other rewards from the work you do.

Meaningful work is a mutual benefit to you and your employer. Your employer wants to capture your engagement, spirit, value, ideas, innovation, and energy. Work can be fun, social, or even cool. Work has meaning. If your employer can help you find meaning at work, it's a mutually beneficial relationship.

Survey data show that emotional engagement of employees and customers is the key to a company's growth and profits. If you're actively engaged with the outcome of what you do, then there's a higher chance that you'll be engaged and find your work meaningful. It's critical to know your meaning of work and is the relationship between what you do, how you do it, and the outcomes you obtain.

Work Lesson Earned: If you aren't engaged in what you do and can't see any relationship between what you do and the outcome, there's a high probability that you won't find meaning at work, ultimately be dissatisfied and move on.

CULTURE RULES

Culture and guiding principles are important to Vucans who work at Microsoft, Apple, Google, We Company, or Nike because they communicate pride and enthusiasm with memorable tag lines. For example, We Company's (formerly We-Work) mission is 'to elevate the world's consciousness'. These mission statements convey to employees that their companies represent caring and excellence, the best companies in their industry.

A number of companies focus on ethics and meaningful work. Space X and Tesla, both founded by Elon Musk, stress the importance of doing life-changing and life-rewarding work. Space X is a commercial space venture. Tesla is an electric automotive manufacturer.

Companies are competing to be family friendly, encourage empowered employees, and respect the dignity of all. Values, culture, principles and ethics are organizational core competencies for success. Organizational core values include respecting individual dignity, integrity, and honesty. Core values are ingrained in the way Vucans act and think. Values then establish direction, guide employees in the right course of action, define challenges, and point to preferred paths.

Kickstarter is a notable company pursuing a higher purpose. The founders decided the crowdsourcing company had met its goals and was making sufficient money. All good. What was the next step? The company rebranded into a Public Benefit Corporation and would focus on the public good instead of going public. The company promises to have an equal number of male and female employees, executive pay less than five times the salary of the average employee, and diversity would be stressed. The company would pursue its social goals and promote its company's values.

Work Lesson Earned: Are these cultural buzzwords reality based? It's important you check these out before moving into a new organization. One of the keys to maintaining work sanity is to understand your employer's culture or customer's values. An organizational culture can empower or kill your career. If you understand and reinforce your customer's or employer's culture, then there's a much higher chance you'll excel. If there's a conflict with your values with those of your employer, deal with it or leave. It's fairly simple. Can you live with the difference? If not, what are the risks and benefits of moving?

AMAZON'S CULTURE AND PRINCIPLES

Companies are designing purposeful and competitive cultures to address disruption. Amazon has it's 14 principles:

1. **Customer obsession.** Employees obsess over customers.
2. **Ownership.** Leaders are shareholders and owners of the company. Workers think long-term and don't sacrifice long-term value for short-term benefits. 'That's not my job' is not part of the Amazon culture.
3. **Invent and simplify.** Leaders require innovation and invention from their teams and all employees with the goal of simplifying processes.
4. **Are right a lot of the time.** Leaders are right a lot of the time because they seek input from diverse workers and perspectives.
5. **Learn and be cautious.** Leaders focus on continuous learning and continuous Improvement.
6. **Hire and develop the best leaders.** Company raises the performance bar for each new hire, team member, and supervisor.
7. **Insist on the highest standards.** Leaders establish and pursue the highest standards of performance and high-quality products.
8. **Think big.** Leaders communicate a bold vision and mission.
9. **Bias for action.** Speed, thought, and action reward winners. Amazon believes in calculated risk-taking and action.
10. **Frugality.** Amazon focuses on doing more with less. Less promotes resourcefulness, self-sufficiency, innovation, and invention.
11. **Earn trust.** Leaders listen, speak candidly, and treat people fairly.
12. **Deep dive.** Leaders operate at all levels of the organization, focusing on details, and establishing tough performance metrics.
13. **Have backbone, disagree, and commit.** Leaders are obligated to challenge decisions and ensure that once a decision is made they commit wholly.
14. **Deliver results.** Leaders focus on performance results including delivering the right products at the right time with high quality.[59]

Work Lesson Earned: Amazon believes in 'purposeful Darwinism'- sort of 'Survival of the Fittest' or 'Shark Tank - Amazon style'? This is real! They reduce headcount by 10% a year to cull under performers. Does your company boast high personal standards? Does your management 'walk the talk.' Then, at what personal cost?

GETTING IT!

The only thing of real importance that leaders do is to create and manage culture. If you do not manage culture, it manages you, and you may not even be aware of the extent to which this is happening.
Edgar Schein – MIT Professor

There's a famous quote that says culture always beats strategy. I once worked for a 'death march' organization. The organization's culture focused on getting projects finished on time and on budget. Those who were on board considered these projects the best work they ever did. For those not on board, these projects, may well have been their worst jobs ever.

I spend a lot of time talking about 'getting it.' 'Getting it' also means understanding your organization's or customer's culture and work rules. I'm an engineer, who sometimes simply didn't 'get it'. Maybe, it was a 'left brain' or 'right brain' thing. Maybe, it was an 'IQ (intelligent quotient) or 'EQ (emotional quotient) thing. I don't know. What I do know after many years of trying to 'get it' and trying different things, I can say that culture is real and those who seem to flow with it do better than those who don't.

Organizational culture is also a matter of attitude. It may be a commitment to listening to customers, designing robust products, manufacturing quality products, or delivering cheerful service. A strong organizational culture develops its own belief systems and language. A culture creates a sense of identity and makes Vucans feel special. Everyone pulling together in the same direction to achieve a common goal engenders organizational unity and strength.

Organizational culture and your personal values should be aligned. Your personal values and morals are the foundations by which organizations and Vucans make choices - where you work, what jobs you do, why you do them, and how you balance family and work. As values are important, organizations recognize they must listen to these concerns or lose valuable employees, the source of new ideas, innovation, and new apps.

Work Lesson Earned: Pay attention to the actions of those who you work with more than their words. If the organizational culture jangles you, then deal with it or it'll kill your career. For example, if a culture is 'dog-eat-dog' competitive and your style is collaborative, you'll be frustrated and eventually leave the organization. Cultural alignment can make or break a career. Learn, adapt, and adopt the culture of your organization or fake it till you make it. If you don't, it'll kill your job and maybe sideline your career.

WHAT'S YOUR GOSPEL OF WORK?

I'm intrigued by what makes a calling. There's a world of difference. Work can simply be a meal ticket or a place to go so other things get done. On the other hand, a calling can be almost spiritual work - work with a higher purpose.

So ask yourself, is your career, job, or work a calling? Does your work drive your passion and purpose? A recent *Atlantic* article calls the Gospel of Work America's new religion. Gospel of Work is where Vucans are finding their identity, self-worth, and success:

> "For the college-educated elite, it (work) would morph into a kind of religion, promising identity, transcendence, and community. ... Some people worship beauty, some worship political identities, and others worship their children. But everybody worships something. And workism is among the most potent of the new religions competing for congregants."[60]

I've known Vucans whose work was a traditional calling. They enjoyed what they did. They solved difficult problems. They made critical decisions. They helped others. They were at the top of their craft. What did these Vucans do? One was an actor, another a policeman, and another was a quality manager. The words they used and how they described their work reveals what makes work a calling. They shared the belief that their work and careers 'made a difference.' While money was important, the work they did and the Vucans they worked with were personally critical to them. In a few cases, the successful outcome was money. They described what they did as their 'passion,' their work partners as 'family,' and workplace as a second home. Other revelations: They ply a craft, not show up for work.

It seems two things are required for workism. First, you must have the God-given ability to do a job and derive enjoyment from it. A calling is unique to each of us, perhaps a match of career, attitude, and aptitude that's made in heaven while tempered on earth. A calling reinvigorates and renews your energies and your perspectives. Finding your interests is the first step to developing a passion for work. With passion comes interest and a willingness to go the extra step for your family or the destitute.

Work Lesson Earned: So, what's your Gospel of Work? What's your passion, purpose, and drivers at work. Can you say that about your job? What tradeoffs or sacrifices would you have to make to find your true calling?

WHAT'S YOUR TRUE NORTH?

The other day, my wife and daughter were out to dinner at a local pizza bar. The place was busy. The server was a tattoo'ed Millennial. The tat across her forearm read: 'Love the process'. Her process was her work. Her passion. Her work affirmation. Maybe, her calling – her true north. True north is a compass metaphor for finding your true path in life and at work.

In much the same way, personal mission statements define who you are and what you do. Vucans believe that personal mission statements are character defining. This is what you do. This is what you won't do.

Work should be meaningful for you. Many friends want to do principle based work in a Green Work World, specifically focused on climate change, sustainability, and green issues. Only a few years ago, I would have said that a lot of companies had principles that were mainly motherhoods and meaningless slogans. With global VUCA, disruptive environmental events are the new normal.

However, things changed for companies in the last decade. Outsourcing and off shoring created a global and integrated economy. Child labor infractions with an offshore supplier could result in reputation loss and subsequent equity loss. Carbon emissions accelerated environmental degradation. And, these gut issues mattered to governments, customers and workers. So, I'm finding that companies are also working to find their true north by paying attention to core principles and values, such as transparency, social responsibility, sustainability, social justice, equity, fairness, and human rights.

On a personal level, my values and principles are critical and sacred. In the same way, work has to be more than money to provide the freedom to do other things. Work is boring unless it has personal meaning or purpose. Work should touch us somewhere. It can be in the pocketbook, heart, and soul.

Work can make the world a better place to live. Work can be challenging and puzzling. Work can get us closer to God. Work can feel just right. Work can be your life's purpose. Work provides meaning, which drives progress, creativity, and progress.

Work Lesson Earned: What's your true north? What do you stand for? What drives you to do the work you do?

WHAT DO YOU STAND FOR?

There are three constants in life... change, choice, and principles.
Stephen Covey

A friend of mine said: 'The most important thing in a worker is character'. OK. Later on I heard the expression: 'Character is destiny'. As I got a little older and did a lot of startups, I got it. A few stories may illustrate this.

I did a mega favor for a person. It was a big deal for me. It was a much bigger deal for the recipient of the favor. I expected a simple 'Thank You.' The person just ghosted me. No communication. No nothing. The person didn't get it. Do you think I'll ever do this again? Yeah!

So, what's going on? Work space may be evolving into war space. Why? Vucans are looking out for #1. New work rules seem as one-sided. And, I'm finding this holy trinity – me, myself and I - in many Vucans, regardless of gender or persuasion. No common courtesy. No return calls. No feedback. No mentoring. No favors. No sharing. No collaboration. Just ghosting. Now, it's reciprocal between Vucan and employer.

Why is this important? Consistent acts of courtesy and kindness are the social lubricant for getting things done at work and through life. The U.S. is coming to the end of a ten year bull economy. In 2020, the U.S. economy may slow down. Employers will have the upper hand. Employers are looking for workers who have high principles, demonstrate common courtesies, and are ethical.

If you don't demonstrate it, you'll be tagged as a high maintenance or worse unethical employee. This is a career killer. The company can always get someone who knows right from wrong, has the common touch, and goes the extra step for customers.

Work Lesson Earned: I'm surprised how many Vucans don't show common courtesy or have the common touch. What do you call this? So, I put this down as lack of self-management. So, how well you manage yourself with good ethics and good principles?

Self-management is a character issue. Your clients and boss pay attention to how you present yourself daily and how you deliver on your promises. Clean up your reputation and YouTube trailers. Your job may depend on it.

STRESS AND ANXIETY – TODAY'S NEW NORMAL

Work to live not live to work.
Anonymous

We've got several startups: 800Compete.com for U.S. infrastructure buildout; WorkingIt.com for the *Future of Work*; CERM Academy for RBPS and RBDM; and Quality + Engineering for Critical Infrastructure Protection: Forensics, Assurance, Analytics®. Why? We don't know which one will pop – think of it as risk diversification.

We work really long hours in these startups. Stress kills. We get it. It sounds like a platitude. Talking about tension, I live it daily. It's heard so often that it seems meaningless. You say: 'OK. I got it, but that's the state of work and state of life these days'. I pay a lot of attention these days to work and job stressors. I think you should too if you're hustling it or doing 996.

Let's look at a few stressors. Many of us are easily distracted with our cell phones and other electronic tools. Many of us have a very hard time concentrating. Attention spans are shrinking.

Execution and stick-to-itiveness are workplace challenges. Vucans often can't concentrate because of distractions. Jobs take much longer. Workers are evaluated in terms of effort and scale, but also back-to-basics criteria such as assessing a person's diligence, goal completion, dealing with failure, and being resilient.[61]

Tech, specifically robotics, machine learning, and artificial intelligence are quickly surpassing our ability to adjust. We've seen that if the tech takes X amount of time to architect, design, and deploy, the people transformation takes five times longer for Vucans to embrace and use new tech. Change is really very painful to the organization.

Work Lesson Earned: Working It in full-time work or side-hustles can be a mirage. We work really hard because we own it, but finding the balance between work and down time can be really hard. Remember, stress Kills. Period. Recognize it. Discuss the issues with your physician, partner, or counselor. Something is going on and it's critical that you find the right balance. Do it now!

GETTING A LIFE!

In matters of style, swim with the current; in matters of principle, stand like a rock.
Thomas Jefferson – U.S. President

It's stunning the number of Vucans who are plain anxious at work. Many suffer from frequent panic attacks. Daily stress is the norm. So, why suffer through this. Again, it's all about self-management and self-care. The number are stunning: "85% of the 1,000 working professionals surveyed report feeling burned out, with 16% of them suffering from burnout every day".[62]

What's happening? Mayo Clinic says: "contributing factors may include a lack of control, unclear job expectations, a dysfunctional working environment and lack of work-life balance."[63] Vucans are quitting their jobs, grudgingly working over-time, and losing the necessary inspiration to contribute ideas. So, many are looking for new work opportunities. This can be a side-hustle for additional monies or a new job.

'Getting a life' is important as workplace tension, work dissatisfaction, horrible boss, and marital conflict increase   And, this is tough for small business and startups. Successful work-family strategies are contentious issues in organizations that try to balance the desires of single people and parents. When a person with children leaves early or can't attend a meeting the burden to get work done falls upon those without similar obligations such as single people. This causes turmoil. What can make a company family friendly? It may involve flex scheduling, job sharing, and stress management counseling.

Companies are simultaneously transforming and want to be 'family friendly.' These two trends sometimes seem incompatible. Each year, companies are competing to be a poster company for 'Best Companies to Work For'. You want flexibility to balance work and family. However, companies want the banner that lists them in the top 100 family friendly companies while the reality is that competitive pressures are increasing.

Work Lesson Earned: Work-life balance is a high stress situation. Deal with it. Before it deals with you with additional stress and anxiety.

HAPPINESS 101

So, first a quick survey: What do you do when your BFF (Best Friend Forever) misses out on a high paying job, gets rejected by an elite school, loses a race, has an outbreak of pimples, etc. What do you think? How do you feel? What do you do? Do you commiserate with the person?

Or, do you have a secret joy of the person's misfortunes? The Germans have a great word for that: Freudenschade, one of those SAT words. Freudenschade translates into 'harm joy'. I think of it as sadistic jealousy and envy from the misfortune of people and even your friends. We're living in Freudenschade age.

So, what do you think Yale University's most popular class ever was? History? Philosophy? Psych 157 or its formal name is 'Psychology and the Good Life'. Expressed another way, the most popular Yale class was Happiness 101. Why? Almost 1/4 of all Yale undergraduates enrolled in the class in its first year. Instructors talked and discussed things, topics, and stories on what Vucans think will make them happy or don't. The critical word is 'think'. How to find happiness in a stressful and unhappy world? Ultimately, the goal and purpose of the class was to teach students how to find, design, and lead a happier life. The Yale instructor noticed:

> "Students want to change, to be happier themselves, and to change the culture here on campus ... With one in four students at Yale taking it, if we see good habits, things like students showing more gratitude, procrastinating less, increasing social connections we're actually seeing change in the school's culture."[64]

Desire for happiness is a sign of times. Even the privileged want to live a better life, find work passion, understand themselves, or be better Vucans.

Work Lesson Earned: Interest in the Yale Psych class and how to find and live the good life went global and viral. Why? Freudenschade. Anxiety. Unhappiness. Envy. In general, there's a happiness deficit around the world in life and work. Grumps, trolls, snarks, and naysayers seem to inhabit the world around us. Recognize these Vucans. Avoid them. And most importantly, get real with yourself. Check out your resting face. If you're one of these Vucans, develop new personal messaging, and practice mindfulness.

LET IT GO!

Look at the resting face of the Vucans next to you. I'll bet their facial expression is hangry (hungry + angry), plain angry, annoyed, irritated, contemptuous, or ... How many faces are smiling? Few or any. It seems that Vucans are negative and flat out grim about their work these days. Maybe it's a sign of the times. Maybe, we're all Vucans living in dystopian times.

The *School of Life* in 'Why The World is Broken' captured the angst:

> "For those of us lucky enough to live through the early 21st century, when unprecedented advancements in medicine, agriculture and technology have rendered many of the evils of the past obsolete, the question remains: why are we still so miserable?
>
> If, as the scientists and academics tell us, our present age is the best possible time to be alive, why do so many yearn to return to an imagined (and illusory) past, whilst others look ahead with horror at a chaotic and doom-laden future?"[65]

Here's the irony. LinkedIn reported that half of U.S. Vucans are disengaged as they're getting fancy titles and promotions with no pay increases. Companies need engagement and productivity from their Vucan employees. However, workers are overwhelmed by tech and automation, which drive up their fears. There's a global anxiety epidemic. Here's a few U.K. statistics:

> "The Mental Health Foundation says that 74% of Brits felt overwhelmed by stress at some point last year, with work being the biggest cause."[66]

Work Lesson Earned: In the U.S. and in many developed areas of the world there's growing anxiety about the impacts and risks of tech on work, careers, and jobs. The anxiety can be seen with rising inequality, gig economy, unemployment, cost of education, and growing divide between what employers want and colleges produce. There's an urgent need to work with these negative thoughts, reframe thinking, and feel mindful about what you do and how you work.

ARE YOU IN THE FLOW ZONE?

'Think in simples' as my old master used to say - meaning to reduce the whole to its parts in simplest terms, getting back to first principles.
Frank Lloyd Wright - Architect

When you're working, 'are you in the flow'? This is the same idea of 'being in the zone' in sports. The answer to this seeming simple question can make the difference between having fun and dreading your work. Read on...

Hungarian psychologist Mihaly Csikszentmihalyi's wrote **Flow** in 1969. He called flow: "the state in which people are so involved in an activity that nothing else seems to matter."[67] He looked at how a person drifted in and out of flow. The preferred work condition was to be in flow. The opposite of flow resulted in boredom, worry, fear, and anxiety, which are words used to describe the current state of work in many parts of the world. In the work flow zone, you lose sense of consciousness including stop internal negative messaging. A person in flow is in control and actively managing what he or she is doing. Time seems to stand still. You gain a sense of managing your time, life, work, and activities.

Csikszentmihalyi believed that work happiness and job satisfaction is all about flow. Happiness results when you're totally absorbed in what you're doing. You don't achieve happiness directly by pursuing it. Happiness results when you forget time and are one with what you're doing.

In athletics, this is called the peak experience. In sports, when a player does a great shot, folks wonder: 'What happened? How did you do that'? The player says: 'I was in the zone'. The athlete feels extraordinarily powerful, relaxed, and potent. If athletes can do it, why can't you do it as well? More time you spend in your flow, the happier you'll be. Check out these flow experiences:

- Clear and doable projects along with feedback on how you're doing.
- Total involvement in the activity that can take you away from your daily worries and frustrations.
- Total concentration or what gives you pleasure without making you self-conscious.

Work Lesson Earned: Are you in the flow zone? Check out how many of the above apply to you? Are you in the zone when you work or in your job?

TOAST AT WORK? – TRY MINDFULNESS

Business has to give people enriching, rewarding lives ... or it's simply not worth doing. **Richard Branson - CEO of Virgin**

Omm ... Stress and anxiety are all around us. Vucans medicate. Vucans exercise. Vucans go to therapy. Vucans meditate. Vucans do mindfulness.

You're always connected, look at the number of Vucans who are driving and texting. Work is a 24 x 7 grind. Work expectations are sky high. Work, family, activities, and interests seem to converge at once. The amount of information you receive is greater than your ability to absorb. Where's the fun? Where's the passion? Where's the gospel of work? Life's too short!

Quite frankly, Vucans are exhausted from the hustle, tired of long hours, and tired of work. Tension kills. It's not fun to be medicated and be out of it. Exercise takes time. Vucans are looking for respite rather than escaping to Burning Man once a year or trekking in Thailand. There has to be a better option.

Mindfulness meditation at work is huge. Work meditation is almost an epidemic as Vucans are using it to induce calm, physical relaxation, and overall wellness. Over the last 20 years, studies have confirmed the health benefits of mindfulness. Mindfulness allows you to focus on the critical things in your life and disconnect from the noise. Companies offer mindfulness workshops and classes. There are a number of the reasons why mindfulness is so popular at home and at work.

Work Lesson Earned: Mindfulness provides an opportunity to learn how to unplug, disconnect, and unwind. Mindfulness can be reframed as stress relief, relaxation, unpacking yourself, self-managing yourself, being in the flow zone, or managing your energy.

Mindfulness is easy. It can be as simple as sitting, counting breaths, and being in the moment. Mindfulness can be as simple as listening to internal messaging. Mindfulness can be relabeled as

LAWS OF LIFE & WORK

Failure is an option here. If things are not failing, you are not innovating enough.
Elon Musk – CEO of SpaceX & Tesla

I like work, career, and job lists. They distill experience. They are a quick read. There's the 'ah ha' moment with things that move you. I can refer to them. Also, they've been vetted and filtered through Vucans' life experiences.

Philip McGraw's **Ten Laws of Life** struck me as write on. I start the book with 'getting it'. By the time, you're through with the book, you'll encounter many if not all of the **Ten Laws of Life** in self-management, RBPS, and RBDM.

Go over each one of these and see which ones fit you.

1. Either you get it or you don't.
2. You create your own experiences.
3. You do what works for you.
4. You cannot change what you do not acknowledge.
5. Work rewards action.
6. There's no reality, only perception.
7. Work is managed, not cured.
8. You teach people how to treat yourself.
9. There's power in forgiveness.
10. You have to name it before you can claim it.

Add the above to your self-management questions.

Work Lesson Earned: 'It is what it is.' If you don't understand or like the 'laws', find out why. If you don't a 'law', do what works for you or in other words 'adopt and adapt for yourself.'

STEPHEN COVEY'S 7 HABITS - STILL WRITE ON!

Watch your thoughts, they become words. Watch your words, they become actions. Watch your actions, they become habit.
Lao Tzu - Chinese Philosopher

In **Working It: Disruption Rules** I've tried to distill work wisdom into a small number of doable takeaways through **Work Lesson Earned**. In the same way, I try to do what Stephen Covey did with his **7 Habits of Highly Effective People**.

The **7 Habits** book has met the test of time. The book has sold 25 million copies and has been translated into 50 languages and is a bestseller after 30 years. We feature it as an example of **Working It** principles.

Covey was probably the most prominent writer promoting the importance of individual values and clarifying the meaning of work. Covey believed that leadership involved creating a culture of shared values and principles.

Take a look at his **7 Habits** and see if they resonate with you:

1. **Be proactive.** Do. Don't stand still. Take the initiative. Be responsible.
2. **Begin with the end in mind.** Projectize your work. Start any activity, a meeting, run, day, or life, with the end in mind. Work to that end and make sure your values are aligned with your goals.
3. **Put first things first.** Develop core practices that help you prioritize your life so you're working on the important stuff.
4. **Think win/win.** Think people and the Golden Rule. Treat Vucans how you want to be treated. This is pretty obvious. You get what you put in.
5. **Seek first to understand, then to be understood.** Develop your core Principles. Listen to emphasize, obtain information, and understand the other person's point of view.
6. **Synergize.** Process and standardize your work so you can scale. Work to create outcomes that are greater than the individual parts.
7. **Sharpen the saw.** Develop your Brand You. Cultivate the essential elements of your character: physical, mental, social/emotional, and spiritual. Expand the essential elements of your mind through continuous learning.

Work Lesson Earned: I think all of Stephen Covey's **7 Habits** are great. Why? They are an inspiration for all of us. The 7P's map closely to the **7 Habits**. What habit do you like the most? What habit do you need to work on?

WORKING IT RULES!

Principles: A basic truth, law, or assumption; a basic source.
American Heritage Dictionary

My personal **Working It** rules distilled from many **Work Lessons Earned** are:

- Action spurs activity from which you can learn (take a risk).
- Do what you hate, first.
- Risks create opportunities in your life and work.
- 80% of life and work involves just showing up (take a risk).
- Go after the upside of life and work – manage downside risk.
- Know your risk appetite and how you make decisions.
- Have a risk plan and direction before you start.
- If the direction you're taking doesn't work for you, then change direction (risk control).
- Focus on the end first and work backwards.
- Focus on the 'critical few' things, not the 'insignificant many'.
- When in doubt, talk with your wife or best friend about it.
- Find the value in what you're doing?
- Finding the meaning in what you're doing, because without it, there's no commitment.
- Pain of changing must be less than the pain of staying the same.
- Structure what you do. Vucans need structure and focus.
- 80% of what worries you will never happen (RBPS/RBDM).

I like these **Working It** rules because they're personal. I've borrowed shamelessly. Some rules and tips are from others. I don't remember where they originated, but I've internalized them and share them with you.

Now do I follow these consistently? I try. I have them in the back of my mind all the time. For example, take a look at the first rule. I'm a worrier. Why? I do risk management. I see the downside in too many things as I do my 'what if' analyses.

Work Lesson Earned: What's your list of **Working It** rules? You know most of the above, but how many do you follow consistently?

ONLY THE PARANOID SURVIVE

Your mind is working its best when you're being paranoid. You explore every avenue and possibility of your situation at high speed with total clarity.
Banksy – Street Artist

A final thought for this section: healthy paranoia is a necessary condition for **Working It**. Paranoia is not a medicated condition. It's not a psychiatric condition. It's simply awareness of current life and work disruptions.

A quick story: Andy Grove, Intel founder and Bill Gates, Microsoft founder were believers in the value of paranoia. Both believed that fear of complacency and stagnation is good for business. Grove said in **Only the Paranoid Survive** that fear is critical for creating and sustaining the passion and energy to win in the marketplace.

Manageable fear is good for the organization, teams, and Vucans. Fear provides the mechanism for overcoming inertia and for stimulating forward movement. Fear can be harnessed and channeled to try harder, do better, and take intelligent risks.

Quick story: Our firm – Quality + Engineering – does risk management. I always seem to asking 'what if?' My wife thinks that I'm always looking at the down side and even seem a little paranoid. I tell her I'm a realist and I've not medicated. I've never been clinically diagnosed as 'paranoid.' So, I put on my happy face until I see another hazard or another 'what if.'

In my world, paranoia is a preemptive insight of what may occur: upside risks (opportunities), downside risks (consequences), black swan events, Murphies, and other unexpected conditions. A strong dose of healthy paranoia is good. I'm not talking about clinical or medicated paranoia. I'm talking about the risk-sensitive paranoia of looking at downside risks and planning on how to mitigate them. Organizational paranoia is good for companies. Personal paranoia is good for you.

These ideas may seem like heresy in today's politically charged world, which says that fear is bad, tension kills, fear causes dysfunctionality, and it makes Vucans go ballistic.

Work Lesson Earned: A friend of mine once said: 'If you're not paranoid, you don't know what's going on' He probably picked this up from the **Only The Paranoid Survive** book, but it sure applies today.

SELF-MANAGEMENT: YOUR NEXT STEPS

- What are your core values?
- What three words describe your core values?
- Is your work a calling?
- What makes you happy?
- What keeps you up at night?
- Are you in the 'flow' at work?
- Do you have a personal vision/mission statement? What is it?
- What matters to you?
- And, why does it matter to you?
- What do you spend your time doing?
- Do these activities add value or happiness or meaning to your life?
- If not, why do you continue doing them?
- What commitments have you made to what Vucans? And why?
- Do you believe these commitments are important to you?
- What things work for you?
- Are you a happy person at work or in general?
- Do you know your organization's culture, vision, mission, or values?
- How do you feel about your organization's culture and values?
- Are your organization's or customer's values aligned with yours?
- Can you live with them if they aren't?
- What do you care about?
- What accommodations regarding values do you make at work and in your life? Any why?
- Can you live with the accommodations?
- Can your employer/customer/stakeholders live with your accommodations?
- What is the one actionable change you would do to enhance your work-life?
- Is your life, work, and family time balanced?
- If not, what can you do about this?
- Do you live your values?

PRACTICES

-

PERSONAL

COMPETENCIES &

WORK HACKS

Principles and Practices work together. Principles focus on knowing the 'why' of your work. Then, Practices focus on knowing and improving the 'how's' of your work. You can think of Practices as Vucan hacks and tools of work.

Machines can do a lot of our rote work. But, our individual creativity and competencies are what differentiates and sets us apart from machines. Vucan creatives may be artists, writers, website builders, drummers, coders, producers, recording engineers, actors, podcasters, and any type of Vucan worker.

As disruption increases, a critical Practice for all Vucans is risk management. Another theme running through this book is each of us will evolve into a risk manager.

VUCAN DRIVERS – PRACTICES

Old Schools	New School
Cause and effect relationships	Interacting relationships
Rear view focused	Future focused
Black and white problems	Shades of gray problems
Where we work	Why and how we work
Normal abilities	Competitive abilities
Work management	Self-management
Work management	Risk management
Risk management professional	Everyone's a risk manager
Externally driven choices	Internally driven choices
FOMO (Fear Of Missing Out) reaction	Hustle culture
Switched on	Switched off & on
Glass is half empty	Glass is redesigned and full
Best decision	Risk-based, decision-making
One solution to a problem	Multiple solutions based on risk
Oral communications	Digital, written, vlog, gif, meme, etc. communications
Emotional reaction	Self-management
Thinking	Doing
Cause and effect	Correlations
Simple questions & problems	Nuanced questions & problems
Regular work	Super jobs with AI, cobots, etc.

PRACTICES @ RISK

Let's look at Paradigms again. Paradigms can be defined in terms of a game. A game has a set of rules, which participants must follow. The game has boundaries such as a basketball court, baseball park, or tennis court.

The game requires specific skills to thrive and practices to compete well. A professional baseball player runs bases; hits a curveball, fastball, slider, and fields a ball. Players keep score. The game score defines winners and losers. We're all Vucans now.   New work, career, and job paradigms require new personal practices and hacks to succeed.

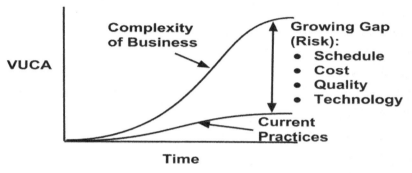

In the above figure, the growing gap between the Complexity of Business and our Current Practices results in schedule, cost, quality, and tech variances or risks. These result in tension, dysfunction, and even fear. If your present practices diverge too much from the complexity of work and current practices, then your work and even employability may be at risk.

If your personal practices are out of date, then sooner than later you'll lose your marketability and employability. As business and work become complex, all of us are losing our ability to keep up. Too much change – too fast – no direction.

Work Lesson Earned: You'll need to evaluate your practices yearly. You'll need to invent new ways of working and even develop productivity hacks. These hacks are your personal practices and productivity habits. To succeed, you'll have to manage your customer, time, quality, communications, risk, tech, and performance commitments. And, you may have to do this on your own time and nickel.

WORKING IT <=> SELF-MANAGEMENT

There's no such thing as time management; there's only self-management.
Rory Vaden – Self-Management Guru and Writer

Vucan managers don't manage in terms of telling a worker what to do, when, and how to do it. Vucan workers are assumed to know their jobs as well as be able to self-manage.

Leaders want to align Vucan's personal needs into the mission of the organization. This can seem like herding cats. If there's no alignment, work won't get done effectively. So, companies have to rely upon workers' maturity and ability to self-manage appropriately to get work done.

Self-management is important to your personal and online life. One mis-step such as a snarky comment can result in your career and work destruction. A single incident such as saying or doing the wrong thing to a person of color, sex, identity, or age can kill a job or a career in a nano-second. A single incident with a significant other can derail a relationship. A misconstrued video, vlog, comment, or selfie can forestall a job interview, promotion, or relationship. So, self-management has evolved into personal risk management.

On-the-job sex has is a critical issue for company executives. All executives are warned to keep their zippers zipped with direct reports. If you get into trouble, don't think that 20 years of great work, promotions, and duty entitles you to anything. Your employer after your lapse in ethics, words, or self-management owes you absolutely nothing – 0, zip, nada.

The common theme throughout this book Is the importance of self-management. Notice I don't use the word self-leadership but self-management, which is doable. The fundamental idea of self-management is that you know how to get things done effectively, economically, and efficiently, but appropriately. You know where the lines are and don't cross then.

Work Lesson Earned: The technical basics of work is IQ driven - getting a project completed within schedule, within cost, and at the right quality level. The behavioral basics of work is EQ driven - knowing where the work lines are and not crossing them without fully understanding the consequences.

DESIGNING A BETTER YOU

Your time is limited, so don't waste it living someone else's life. Don't be trapped by dogma - which is living with the results of other people's thinking. Don't let the noise of others' opinions drown out your own inner voice. And most important, have the courage to follow your heart and intuition.
Steve Jobs – Apple Founder

Self-improvement has always been a hot topic. Books are written. Podcasts are uploaded. Design thinking is the hot new method of developing self-management practices. It goes like this:

The *Wall Street Journal* recently asked in an article: 'Is Design Thinking The New Liberal Arts'? You may think of design as what an engineer does with a product or an architect does for the building. Yes, but it's more.

Design thinking is a new way to do work and live. Design thinking is used in education, systems, entrepreneurship, business strategies, science, art, and making a better you.

Can design thinking create a 'better and happier you'? The 'better you' may be a healthier lifestyle, better habits, increased productivity, higher agility, solved problems, or better decisions. Or expressed another way, can workers consciously design their life, work, career, or job? Maybe, yes!

Work Lesson Earned: The common theme of many self-help books is a form of design thinking to create better habits or get unstuck.

Design thinkers believe the following design practices can help you be a better person and get important things done in your life:

1. Understand the context of a problem.
2. Define the final problem so it is understandable and solvable.
3. Ideate, make lists, write down ideas, brainstorm, identify risks, or identify anything that may prevent you from reaching an objective.
4. Create a plan to solve the problem or make a decision.
5. Test the solution (s) and get feedback from others.

Give these a try! They may help you.

WORKING IT SUCCESS

Quick question: What do you think is more important to career success - people skills or technical skills? Both as it turns out. Bell Labs studied emotional quotient, the EQ, and found it is as important to your long-term success as your IQ. IQ, the Intelligence Quotient, was once prized to be the key to career success. So, emotional and behavioral management is another key element of self-management.

We can see this with Gen-Zer's – the first full-on digital generation. They may have the lowest EQ, social maturity, and communications ability of any generation. Gen Z's were born between 1995 and 2010. They've used, learned, socialized, and worked with smart phones since birth. If you're in doubt, talk to any young person who has been hovering over his or her smart phone for over 20 years. Their EQ can be abysmal as interactions with this generations demonstrate.

EQ includes: grit, passion, likeability, communications, drive, and motivation, which are important work and life success factors. Many motivated average or less than average IQ people have excelled in life and work through focused desire and drive.

Work Lesson Earned: So, what does success have to do with smarts? I know middling intelligent Vucans who've made it big. Some wrote best-selling mystery books, designed killer products, built a killer app, or sold real estate. Some of these Vucans seem like they belonged in Densa not Mensa, the genius organization. What did they all share? High EQ with risk-taking and grit.

Each of us has one or multiple core competencies or practices. Smart Vucans in life learn to identify, develop, and capitalize them. What's critical to your life and work success? What does success mean to you? Success goes beyond intelligence. So, understand what it takes to excel in your field or profession.

SELF-MANAGEMENT MATTERS

Change the things that can be changed, accept those that cannot, and have the wisdom to know the difference.
Serenity Prayer

Vucan leadership often surfaces in a battle or fiscal emergency, where the consequences of poor judgment are fatal. We believe that critical self-management issues will surface for each of us in opportunity situations (upside risk) and high consequence situations (downside risk).

Most of us think about and look at downside risk, such as Murphies, bad events, or bad things. Let's look at opportunity situations (upside risk). For example, can risk-based, problem-solving (RBPS) and decision-making (RBDM) make a difference in a business organization or a project team? Studies indicate that Vucan leadership is shown in teams and small organizations. Small product development teams have developed breathtaking products, project teams have constructed wonders of the world, and small combat teams have changed the outcome of battles and even wars. In these instances, leader's made smart decisions in VUCA time that had a dramatic impact on organizational performance.

A simple business example illustrates the power of Vucan leadership. The captain of a fishing vessel can be a leader who makes a noticeable difference. A fishing vessel is a unique environment. It's a mobile small business similar to a food truck whose success is determined by its catch of fish. It's isolated from many influences. It's self-contained and can be studied. One study found that 40% of the variation in the herring catch among boats in the country's fishing fleet depended on the personality of the captain.

A similar survey of top U.S. and Canadian companies concluded that 15 to 25% of the variation in a company's profitability was directly due to their chief executives. Fishing boat captains sense where the fish are and executives know where the money is!

Work Lesson Earned: Organizations are looking for workers and requiring contractors to self-manage their work, be innovative, and make their numbers.

EXECUTION UPSIDE AND DOWNSIDE

We have a strategic plan. It's called 'doing' things.
Herb Kelleher - Founder Southwest Airlines

I personally don't like the word 'execute.' It's negative. It implies a very unforgiving downside. However, get used to it. You'll be hearing it often.

A little story may help explain the term. Most consultants, managers, and executives are fond of planning. Planning is high level and strategic. Planning is antiseptic. Planning is theoretical and hypothetical. Planning is removed from operations. Planning is removed from people. And, planning is fun.

In contrast, execution is almost the opposite. Execution is the application of best practices. Execution is ground level and tactical. Execution is real and tied directly to innovation, cost reduction, and profitability. Execution is operational. Execution is emotional. Execution is through people and very personal. Execution can be messy, dirty, and not so fun. What do you think is more valuable to executive management: planning or execution? Duh? Planning is a cost center. Execution is a profit center.

Managing, organizing, commercializing, and monetizing are keys to competitiveness. It's all about execution - creating value and wealth. In our digital world, new ideas and knowledge dominate value-adding product design, process improvement, and project completion mix. And, commercializing and monetizing the innovation through flawless execution is the new Vucan work paradigm.

The flip side of execution management is knowledge management. By executing and innovating, you develop proprietary and intellectual property (IP). Ariel de Geus, a management strategist, once said "the ability to learn faster than your competitors may be the only sustainable competitive advantage."[68] Applied innovation and protected knowledge add value. These allow the smartest organization to execute, specifically to deliver products and services faster and better than its competitors do.

Work Lesson Earned: A critical theme throughout this book is the emphasis on doing – RBPS and RBDM execution. While breakthrough ideas that can be monetized are important, the deployment of the ideas along with monetization are critical to any startup and side-hustle.

MONEY, MONEY, MONEY ...

Here's a test? When you look at a work, job, or career opportunity, do you see calamity or opportunity. Is the glass half full or half empty? Or, do you want to design a new glass container and fill it with your fluid of choice? The latter is the key question and attribute of all entrepreneurs, do'ers, makers, and creators.

It's all about how you see your world. It's your lens. It's your work framework. So, what's your life and work lens? The pessimist sees the glass as half empty. The optimist sees it as half full. The dreamer, risk taker, and founder see it as a new glass that you design and fill with your stuff.

So, let's talk level of effort, execution, and money. Jack Ma, China's Elon Musk, believes that the future of Chinese global innovation, competition, and domination is based on the '996' system of work. The west has the '9 am to 5pm' work paradigm. China has shifted the west's paradigm to the '996' system of work from '9 am to 9 pm six days a week'.

Jack Ma, founder of Alibaba, and Richard Liu, founder of JD.com, go so far to say that 12-hour work days are a 'blessing.' And, work 'slackers' are risks both to their firms and to the vision of Chinese global economic domination.[69] Tough Vucan messaging for developing dominant work models in disruptive times.

What's happening in China, India, Vietnam and many countries of Asia? No privilege. Just Vucans who work 996 and want to invent their own glass. Think domination through innovation. Does it work? Well, China has more billionaires than any other country. So, the west bemoans 'balance of work and life.' The west bemoans privilege, social injustice, and unfairness. China wants their **Working It** hustlers owning the *Future of Work*.

Work Lesson Earned: Those of us tied to old paradigms may feel confused, uncertain, and even pain on the 'show me da money' focus. Many say it's unfair and want Universal Basic Income (UBI) and socialism. What do you think of UBI?

You can clutch at the old paradigm or flow with the new one. It's not a matter of seeing the glass as half full or half empty. Both are static, 'so what' choices. The smart option may be to see a new glass so it can be filled with your beverage of choice. This risk-taking choice is proactive, opportunistic, and entrepreneurial. It's the same with your career. Do you want to seize career and work opportunities, take risks, and design your own glass? It's your call!

YOU ARE YOUR CHOICES

All business proceeds on beliefs or judgments of probabilities, and not on certainties.
Charles Eliot - President Harvard University

Decision-making in VUCA time is changing. Fashionable acronyms are coined for today's dominant decision-making paradigms, which seem to be fear and anxiety based. Let's look at a few:

FOMO, the Fear Of Missing Out, is a popular decision-making option. It means that workers are continuously searching for and fearing not being part of the next big thing, great experience, investment opportunity, or social interaction.

FOBO, the Fear Of Better Options, means that Vucans can't make a final decision because they relentlessly pursue the dream of capturing and experiencing all options. This eventually leads to decision paralysis and huge regret.

FODA, the Fear Of Doing Anything, is a do-nothing approach to Vucan decision-making based on anxiety. This is the same as risk avoidance. We've all been in this position. You've seen the thousand-yard stare or the deer-in-the-headlights look. You've seen these Vucans and may be ourselves in these situations. Fear is overwhelming. You don't have enough information. You don't believe you can make a good decision. You're overwhelmed with data. There are too many unknowns and unknowables. So what do you do? Nothing. Sometimes, anything.[70]

Work Lesson Earned: FOMO, FOBO, and FODA are real for Vucans. They are nervous and reactive forms of decision-making. They don't result in good choices. Jay Samit in **Disrupt You** said: "Disruption isn't about what happens to you, its' about how you respond to what happens to you". [71]

Your career management in the *Future of Work* should be based on making smart choices. Ask yourself: are you: 1. Risk-taking; 2. Risk-sensitive; or 3. Risk-averse? Each of these is a specific lens or filter that may bias, color, or distort your vision of life, work, career, and job. One may not be better than another. It is what it is. If you don't think you're one of these, what do you think may be your risk filter?

VUCAN DECISION TIPS AND TOOLS

I am not a product of my circumstances. I am a product of my decisions.
Stephen Covey – Educator & Writer

Life and work are all about making smart choices - specifically risk-based, problem-solving (RBPS) and deciding (RBDM). And quite frankly, it sucks for most Vucans. It's not easy. Why? Because many of our decisions are reactive, impulsive, or stimulus driven below our threshold of awareness. Or, in other words, most of the time we aren't aware of what we're doing and deciding. Let's call this the fog of life and work.

We're big believers in choice. We've had discussions with Vucans without marketable skills, which are based on poor personal problem-solving and decision-making. Let's look at a few examples: If you got a degree in a non-marketable area, it was your decision. If you took out lots of school loans, it was your decision. If you haven't upgraded your skills, it was your decision.

What's the solution? Where does one start? We think that it starts with self-awareness, self-acknowledgement, and self-management.

Let's look at money skills. Financial risk education is required in 19 U.S. states. Many colleges are starting financial literacy programs. Harvard and Princeton had their first finance workshops this year complete with T-shirts and consultations. The Harvard economics professor that instructed the class said: "There are long-term trends like the increase in inequality, rising student debt, that make students very mindful of the challenges they are going to face."[72]

Work Lesson Earned: So, what's the solution? The below quote is from a *Business Week* article: 'What Happens When an Economist Walks into a Brothel' provides a few clues:

> "To learn how to manage risks in your life, don't consult office-bound economists or actuaries. Ask the real experts: prostitutes, gamblers, magicians, paparazzi, big-wave surfers, movie producers, horse breeders, and soldiers. Their careers require them to take risks. They succeed by doing so smartly—deriving as much benefit as possible per unit of risk taken."[73]

YOU'RE NOW A RISK MANAGER

The essence of risk management lies in maximizing the areas where we have some control over the outcome while minimizing the areas where we have absolutely no control over the outcome.
Peter L. Bernstein – Risk Author

We're all Vucans. This implies that each of us is inherently a risk manager. Why? Maybe, it's hard wired into our DNA. Look at the 'fight or flight' syndrome our ancestors had to live and decide by. The very survivability of our species was defined by this simple risk-based conundrum. Recently, Travis Bradberry in *Forbes* said: "The real obstacle to positivity is that our brains are wired to look for and focus on threats."[74] Let's look at a few threats and risks:

If you pick up any paper or listen to any TV show, about three quarters of the programs deal with risk. Risk is the lens for most of our work. The good thing is that a risk lens can be developed and adaptability can be learned.

Risks can result from cyber-attacks, food recalls, theft, violence, crossing the street, and then the mother of all risks the possible extinction of humans from climate change. Extinction may come from multiple sources. Meteor strike. Super volcano eruption. Global warming. Nuclear war. Robogeddon. Influenza. In other words, there're too many risks to count.

VUCA messaging and fears in our heads is also causing real tension. Most of us want certainty and control in our lives. However, we destroy ourselves worrying about everything. FOMO. Every decision is fraught with risk. Everything is a problem that can't be solved. So, there are lots of advice givers. Executives have personal coaches. Vucans talk about day-to-day challenges. Bosses give Millennials daily or weekly feedback and suggestions and how to improve.

Work Lesson Earned: Vucans want stability not volatility, certainty not uncertainty, simplicity not complexity, and clarity not ambiguity. In other words, Vucans want the opposite of VUCA. Vucans want predictability, consistency, and safety. Vucans will have to develop new habits and learn how to deal with disruption and risk.

YOUR RISK PROFILE

Two roads diverged in a yellow wood, ...
Robert Frost – Author of *The Road Not Taken* Poem

What roads have you taken in life and work? Did you have choices of multiple roads? Why did you make the choices you made? Or, did circumstances dictate the choice for you? How did you look at risk? These simple questions may help define your happiness in life and work. The more choices you had, the smarter the decisions you made, the higher the probability you're happy.

From our experience, your personal risk profile or risk appetite is one of the key factors in determining your life's work arc and ultimately your satisfaction. Do you know your risk appetite or tolerance? You may be risk-taking, risk tolerant, or risk-averse. Let's try to explain.

Why do you keep doing the same things over and over again that don't make you happy? One reason: you may be risk-averse. Or, you may feel comfortable by taking the well-traveled and familiar road in the above quote. It's natural. Most of us take the path of least resistance because it's a known and well-trodden path. And, much of life works this way. This is OK for most work decisions.

A risk taker would aim for the higher rewards that come with taking higher risks. Risk-sensitive Vucans may be the smartest. They don't want to lose what they have by taking the unknown road leading to more risk.

Most of us are not one or the other, we assume different roles and make decisions based on context. A risk-averse Vucan would probably want a full-time job with an established corporation, preferably doing core work. And, a risk-sensitive Vucan would be a gig-worker when the economy is expanding and a full-time employee when the economy is contracting for stability. Another interesting element of work decision-making is we tend to look for facts that support our thinking (confirmation bias) and disbelieve messages that don't conform our thinking.

Work Lesson Earned: How do you make decisions and choices on your work/career? Do you tend to hang on and do the same thing even when you have contrary or warning messages? Do you make random choices because you fall into work because it was available? Or, is it reactive since it is the path of least resistance? Or, is it situational and tactical since you like to solve problems and make optimal decisions.

RISK-BASED, PROBLEM-SOLVING & DECISION-MAKING

I think we now live in an era when many of the concerns in running organizations are being reframed in terms of risk, which suggests that risk professionals are likely to rise to the top.
Harvard Business Review

In **Against the God: The Remarkable Story of Risk**, the author says the mastery of risk is the foundation of modern life and is what divides modern humans from ancient times. So, the logic flow in **Working It** goes like this: VUCA => Disruption => Risk => RBPS/RBDM => Self-Management

Let's unpack these ideas. So, what is risk management? The dictionary defines risk as the "potential for the realization of unwanted negative consequences of an event."[75] Murphy is alive and well - if something bad can happen it will. You can try to understand and mitigate Murphies or they can victimize you. The choice is yours. Risk management is the practice how you minimize the impacts of Murphies from crossing a street to starting a business. Why do you bother looking both ways when you cross a street? You look for possible sources of risk like a truck pancaking you.

By consciously or unconsciously calculating probabilities, you make intelligent decisions and take control of your life. As discussed, this is called RBPS and RBDM. RBPS and RBDM are fundamental elements of all work from a hustling startup to a traditional organizational culture. RBPS is the ability to develop products that Vucans want. RBDM is the consistent ability and agility to make reliable decisions.

You don't have to make a conscious risk assessment in all situations but can intentionally and intuitively look at alternatives at how you work day-to-day. When you're confident of an outcome, you decide it's the right thing to do. Rightness comes when there's risk congruence with your heart, head, and gut about risks that's acceptable to you.

Work Lesson Earned: As the world is becoming interconnected, Murphies are just waiting to occur. Understand risk management. Add it to your professional tool kit. Read risk books: **Black Swan** and **Against the Gods: The Remarkable Story of Risk**.

VUCAN RISK FRAMEWORKS

A framework is a lens to describe RBPS and RBDM. ISO 31000:2018, an international standard, is a simple risk framework. Risk management, both upside and downside, can be defined as the ability to reach an objective, solve a tough problem, or make a smart decision. ISO 31K has the following steps:

- **Communicate and Consult.** You solve problems or make decisions because someone has an itch, pain, need, want, expectation, perception, or requirement. Understanding and figuring out what problem to solve, what pain needs to be relieved, or what itch needs to be scratched is the first step in the RBPS and RBDM journey. This step explains what problem we are trying to solve, why we are solving it, how we may go about solving it, and how to make a decision.

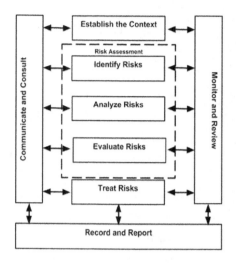

- **Establish the context:** Years ago, I was told understanding context is worth 20 IQ and EQ points. Context provides understanding of the importance, meaning, purpose, and value of the problem to be solved or decision to be made. Context allows us to process the right information, understand risks, analyze events, perceive obstacles, understand Vucans, learn from mistakes, and do the right things to meet the objectives. This is a critical point because the human ability to nuance context separates us from smart machines — at least for now.

- **Identify risks:** Think of risks as hurdles, impediments, or obstacles that are in the way of a finishing a project, reaching an objective, solving a problem, or making a critical decision. There are lots of risks. It's critical to separate the critical few risks from the insignificant many that get in the way of what you want to do. So, pay attention to what matters.

- **Analyze risks:** Risk analysis involves understanding the type, extent, and nature of the risk and obstacle to solve a problem or make a decision. Think of risk in terms of two factors: likelihood of the event and possible consequences. RBPS and RBDM consider both positive and negative consequences. Risk analysis is critical to determine if a problem can be solved or decision be reached. RBDM was relatively straight forward a dozen years ago. Risk likelihood and consequences could be evaluated fairly simply. Many problems had a cause and effect relationship. A or B or C would cause D. Systems are now very complex with dependencies, interdependencies, cascading, and other factors.

- **Evaluate risks:** Risks are always evaluated based on an organization's or Vucan's risk appetite or tolerance. Risk tolerance is the acceptable level of variation a company or individual is willing to accept in the pursuit of a specific objective. As a recommendation, if there's residual risk beyond your tolerance or appetite additional risk mitigation might be applied.

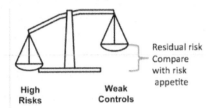

High Risks   Weak Controls

Residual risk Compare with risk appetite

- **Treat risks:** Risk treatment involves 4 RBDM options: 1. Avoid; 2. Accept; 3. Transfer; or 4. Reduce or Control the risk. Let's look at each: Risk avoidance, think FODA, is the decision not to do something. Risk acceptance, think go-for-it, is the decision to do something usually because it's acceptable to your risk tolerance. Risk transference assumes someone else may assume part of the risk. Risk management or control, think FOBO, is the decision to reduce the risk through eliminating obstacles, reducing likelihood or reducing consequences.

- **Record and Report:** This step involves sharing your RBPS and RBDM with critical parties such as your significant other.

- **Monitor and Review:** VUCA changes. Risks change. So, risks have to be monitored and reviewed all the time.

Work Lesson Earned: Add RBPS and RBDM to your LinkedIn profile and resume. It'll give you a leg up in your job competition.

ADAPTATION AND RESILIENCE

VUCA is a continuous process that results in increasing disruption over time. Automation, machine learning, artificial intelligence, Internet of Things, and many technologies are advancing faster than our abilities to understand and cope. Companies have to adapt. Vucans have to be resilient. Some companies and Vucans can adjust well, others can't or won't.

So, what to do? Disruptor companies will have strengths which may involve IP, costing, people, tech, or process advantages. The disruptee company will have to respond to the comparative advantages of the disruptor or be toast.[76]

Legacy and disruptee companies have established paradigms and processes that inhibit innovation and new behaviors. Like moving a mega container ship, large companies can't pivot like startups that can develop new products and services and market them rapidly.

It comes down to people. Interesting phenomenon we've seen is Human Resource organizations have rebranded to talent organizations. Companies are realizing that new ideas come from Vucans and creatives are critical to a company's sustainability, competitiveness, and profitability. So what you're seeing is a new class of creatives with special talents being paid a premium.

Work Lesson Earned: So, what can companies do to be nimble and entrepreneurial in the *Future of Work*? Over the next 5 years, all companies are developing effective change and sustainable business models. There is no management guru pointing the way or offering tips on adaptation and resiliency. Possible steps may involve:

1. Challenge work and business model assumptions.
2. Create a team to help lead the effort.
3. Define the organization's vision of the *Future of Work*.
4. Communicate the new vision of the *Future of Work* to all stakeholders.
5. Experiment and empower workers to act as startups.
6. Implement broad based change carefully.[77]

COMMUNICATING – THE LOST SKILL

How well we communicate is determined not by how well we say things but by how well we are understood.
Andrew Grove, CEO Intel

Think of the last dinner you had in a restaurant where most couples were using smart phones to keep current, contact friends, and text their date 2 feet away. It's worse when digital natives communicate and text almost exclusively through smart phones.

The mega problem: Good communications are a vital element to all work problem-solving and career decision-making. Communications problems can impact senior executives to low-level workers. You may remember as little as 25% of what you heard in the last two days. Poor listening results in the wrong coffee order, poor quality instructions, and even incorrect medical procedures. Can you imagine scheduled for an appendix removal and lose your lung instead? That would make for a bad appendix day. Strange things happen and result in massive medical liability awards because of poor communications!

For example take GE, which is in tough shape. Poor risk-based decisions. Poor risk-based, problem-solving. So, they are in disruptee mode. The CEO needs to be consistent and transparent in all communications. He recently said the turnaround will take years and "I don't want to sugar coat that in any way, shape or form. There's a lot of work. It's a game of inches."[78] Simply said. Pretty clear. Gotta get'er done.

Poor communications is a huge problem with Vucans and digital natives. Big problem at work and in life. If your personal vision, mission, values, culture, goals, plans, policies, and procedures are not uniformly understood, then they won't be followed. It all comes down to understandable communications. It's that simple. Poor decisions are made. Processes won't work. Projects aren't completed. Deficient products are produced. And, ultimately unhappy customers won't purchase products or services.

Good communications starts with good listening. The problem is Vucans are texting and listening less. No wonder communication, or the lack of it, hampers our work effectiveness and even relationship happiness.

Work Lesson Earned: So, what separates leaders from managers, great creatives from so-so workers, million dollar-a-year professionals from commodity consultants? Killer listening and great communications.

TECHNOLOGY – LEARN TO LOVE IT

As technology advances in complexity and scope, fear becomes more primitive. **Don DeLillo – Writer.**

I'm surprised how many Vucans are techno-phobes in a tech-economy.

Wonder why? When you hear the following words, what do you think about? Faster. Better. Killer. Cheaper. Smaller. Agile. Tech and specifically the smart phone are usually at the heart of disruption. Tech both drives and facilitates this change. Futurist Alvin Toffler called this shift to an information or knowledge-based society the **Third Wave**.

Moore's law is the cornerstone of electronic goods as they're cheaper, faster, and better. How fast is this occurring? Computer power keeps increasing as the cost of computation falls. Moore's Law: computers and cell phones that double their capacity, performance, or capability every two years or cost half as much.

Tech has done much good. But, many of us haven't adapted well. Americans are overwhelmed at work more than two years ago. The reasons vary. Stakeholder and customer expectations are increasing. Tech is speeding up work. Managers and supervisors use tech to monitor and control work output. Tech drives organizational transformations. Tech is difficult to keep up with.

Tech is critical with digitalization and transformation. Management leverages tech to coordinate the overall direction of teams, ensure there's alignment with the overall strategic direction, balance corporate resources, and ensure stakeholder requirements are understood and satisfied.

Work Lesson Earned: So, learn to love tech. There's no escaping using tech at work and in your life. Technophobia is the fastest way to ensure your professional obsolescence and even unemployment.

INNOVATE OR GET OBLITERATED

We're in the age of the idea. The organizations that can develop a culture of creativity and idea generation will be the winners.
Kevin Roberts - CEO, Saatchi & Saatchi

We're all knowledge workers. "Knowledge workers have high degrees of expertise, education, or experience, and the primary purpose of their jobs involves the creation, distribution, or application of knowledge."[79]

Innovation is an interesting concept. I'm an engineer and have designed power plants, software, and many products. Every time I was on a project I thought I was innovating. Innovation can be seen as incremental improvement, breakthrough design, or disruptive change.

I think that personal innovation is the key to self-management and career survivability over the next ten years because of the half-life of information and careers. Every discipline, function, and career has a shorter half-life. Half-life is the length of time information, or data doubles in a profession. The half-life of knowledge in electrical engineering or computer science may be 3 or 4 years. In medical specialties, it may even be shorter. Workers who don't update their knowledge, skills, and abilities are prone to professional obsolescence or at worst functional toast.

Knowledge is applied. How many of us are knowledge workers? It's estimated that a quarter to half of all Vucans in North America are knowledge workers, who develop and manipulate information. These Vucans provide the economic value and are the most critical workers to a company. Companies with the most knowledge workers usually have the highest market capitalization.

Applied knowledge is the great business differentiator and value-adder inside companies. Knowledge management may mean identifying and internalizing best practices; correcting and preventing discrepancies; fault proofing the organization; and commercializing new ideas. This asset while not on the financial books is critical to profitability as companies want to accelerate product development and profits from new products.

Work Lesson Earned: If you're a professional who does not keep current with your profession or specialty, then you'll be functionally illiterate and maybe unemployable. Think 'Moore's Law' for professionals.

SELF-MANAGEMENT - YOUR NEXT STEPS

- Who are your direct customers and stakeholders?
- How do you satisfy your customer and stakeholders?
- How do your customer know and measure the value of your contributions?
- Is your work value-adding? How?
- How is your value measured and monetized?
- Are you risk-taking, risk-sensitive, or risk-averse?
- Can you describe how your risk nature impacted your decisions?
- What would you do different knowing what you know now?
- Do you have a high, low, or no tolerance for failure? Why or why not?
- How does your customer or boss value your contributions?
- What are your time constraints?
- How do you manage your time around these constraints?
- What does quality mean to you and your stakeholders?
- Are you a good communicator?
- How do you manage work/career risk?
- How do you keep up with tech?
- Are you finding yourself restless and can't relax?
- Do your wife, friends, or significant other worry about you?
- Do you get angry easily?
- Do you get tired or frustrated easily?
- Do you have difficulty concentrating?
- Are you putting on or losing a lot of weight?
- Have you lost interest in your usual recreational activities?
- Are you worried about things that you can't control?
- Are you having trouble concentrating?
- Do you work long hours?
- Are you sleeping longer, almost escaping things that you have to do?
- Do you feel that you're in control or out of control?

PRODUCTS

-

THE BRAND YOU

The Products part of the 7P's framework is based on discovering your 'what' of work and then help you define your 'who' of work.

This section first addresses the organizational and then personal elements of Products. Each organization makes products using the latest technology. In the front of this section, we describe the biggest disruptors to work including artificial intelligence, machine learning, Internet of Things, and smart machines.

Then, we discuss personal element of products. Each of us has a personal brand much like each business has a business brand. You already know what the Apple brand stands for. So, we discuss what personal brands stand for. Your personal brand is your product - YOU. As companies are disrupted, Vucans are impacted. Much like any product needs to be updated with a new design, features, and capabilities, you'll have to update your personal practices.

Your personal brand is not only reputation, but it's more Personal branding is not only your value add and best personal practices, but your core principles specifically in terms of what you believe in. You need to know what you stand for to live and work authentically

VUCAN DRIVERS - PRODUCTS

Old School	New School
Product based, 'brick and mortar' business model	Platform based, online business model
You are your work	You are Brand You
Ping pong table @ work	High salary & meaning @ work
Compete individually to succeed	Collaborate as team to succeed
Traditional company stability	Startup risk
Good salary + benefits	IPO
Company office	Telecommute or co-working space
Machines are industrial robots	Machines are co-bots etc.
Robots take jobs in 20 years	Robots take jobs next year
Robots can't learn	Robots can learn, nuance, and adapt
Ivy league & branded degree is every thing	Engineering degree with AI/ML emphases
Machined and mass assembled products	3-D printed products and prostheses
Full time employment	Gig-work nation
Average is good enough in everything	Best in class in a few areas
Risk aversion	Risk-taking
Homesteading	Hustling and crushing it
Disruptee	Disruptor
Look out for the employer	Look out for #1
Static business models	Agile business models

PRODUCTS & ROBOTS @ RISK

Current robots are only able to replace people in very limited circumstances. And people don't want to work in factories. They want more comfortable jobs. That is what happens when standards of living and education rise. All people everywhere aspire to better lives.

Rodney Brooks- Robot Engineer

Quick robot joke? A textile mill has been automated. The mill only has two employees: a man and a dog. The man is there to feed the dog. The dog is there to keep the man away from the machines. This joke in various forms is repeated in terms of the impact of automation and robotics on almost all types of work.[80] Like all jokes, there's a grain of truth and even revelation in it.

Robot memes: Bots are coming. They've landed. They are impacting all work. Bots will take over repetitive work. They may take or at least change your job. This has been a fear based meme since the Terminator movies.

To blunt robot and Terminator stereotypes, personal robots look laughably friendly to increase our acceptance of them and sound approachable. Think of Alexa and Siri bots. We're pretty much used to their voices and what they can do. Robots may help our kids solve math problems. Cobots can work with us on critical decision-making. Home bots can clean our homes. Factory bots can lift heavy objects and do our dangerous work. Bots can motor you around as you get older. Killer bots can fight our wars.

The tech friendly believe that robots will end repetitive work and create opportunities for creative work. There will be time to provide an individualized services such as school tutoring or working with the homeless. Work will be disrupted and give us more free time, but with fewer workers.

Work Lesson Earned: In this section, we offer a lot of predictions – sometimes grim. For example, McKinsey Global Institute estimates that up to a third of the American workforce will have to switch to new occupations, not jobs, by 2030.

The reality is no one really knows what the robotic future will look like. Dystopia? Utopia? What I do know is that companies, governments, society, and Vucans are not ready for the coming changes.

INTERNET OF THINGS (IOT)

A year ago when I talked to truck drivers they said 'there's no way a robot could do my job.' This year they say, 'We need to make robot trucks illegal'.
Andrew Yang - 2020 US Presidential Candidate

Last year, I was working on a suspense book, that had a smart killer toaster. Too cheeky. Well, read on.

I needed an IOT thing such as an office product or a killer toaster that could be hacked, cause a fire, and kill the occupants. Refrigerator was too big and couldn't figure out how to make it into a killing machine. We know that smart reefers have smart tags to measure spoilage rates, what food to order automatically, and what food to toss due to its spoilage date. The toaster was a better choice because it could be accessible, hacked, short circuited, and cause a fire.

The bad news! Bots are coming sooner than expected. Intelligent machines will take over a lot of repetitive jobs within 5 years - a lot sooner than anyone predicted. Not good!

Homes, offices, buildings, and factories already full of smart machines (robots) are able to communicate with each other on their own. And this is not stopping. Tiny computers and systems will be embedded in objects such as the smart toaster, our clothes, or smart refrigerator. While, we have smart factories with robotic welders and pick/place robots. Smart buildings can automatically adjust the heating, ventilation, and air conditioning to individual rooms based on the number of Vucans in the room. This is called the Internet of Things or Internet of Everything.

The smart world will impact everything. Autonomous vehicles will be able to drive Vucans in personal vehicles and deliver products. Autonomous pilots will fly cargo planes and a few years later commercial aircraft. What about passengers? Well, the online pilot much like trucks and a physician will provide the requisite peace of mind (think risk assurance) that a human is in charge

Work Lesson Earned: This bears repeating. This is survival time for companies. Companies have to innovate, invent, and compete. In much the same way, Vucans will need to keep up and develop complementary, competitive skills.

The question: 'What's the role of people gonna be in VUCA time'? What are Vucans' going to be and do? What are the new work rules? No easy answers.

RACE AGAINST THE MACHINE

Automation will force us to realize that we are not defined by what we do.
Kai-Fu Lee - President of Google China

Cars are already computers on wheels. And in the next stage in the automotive journey, cars will be robots on wheels similar to Transformers.

I saw a movie the other day about robots. The critical question in the movie: 'Was the robot sentient or in other words, could it feel and think like a human'? Kinda like an advanced Turing robot. Nice idea!

Critical questions are: 'Can robots solve problems and make smart decisions like us'? A few years ago, smart machines were only able to make simple calculations and decisions based on programmed instructions. If an opportunity was presented that was outside of these instructions, then the machine really could not make a decision or solve a problem as the following reveals:

> "Today's robots can perform only limited reasoning due to the fact that their computations are carefully specified. Everything a robot does is spelled out with simple instructions, and the scope of the robot's reasoning is entirely contained in its program. Furthermore, a robot's perception of its environment through its sensors is quite limited. Tasks that humans take for granted – for example, answering the question, 'Have I been here before?' - are extremely difficult for robots ... it is work for a machine to differentiate between features that belong to a scene it has already observed and features of a new scene that happens to contain some of the same objects."[81]

Work Lesson Earned: So, here's the conundrum. The above quote is only 3 years old. Several points in the above quote are no longer true. Robots have cognitive capabilities and smarts than even AI experts have not anticipated. With additional computing power and neural network smarts, the machines can gather data and make predictions based on pattern recognition. Robots are already making some careers obsolete. So, is your work vulnerable?

THE MACHINES ARE LEARNING FASTER

'Workers, Your Robot Overlords Have Arrived.'
Wall Street Journal article headline

"It's time to stop worrying that robots will take our jobs – and start worrying that they will decide who gets a job." [82] This is the lead sentence in the above WSJ article. Fear mongering? Or reality? Or, a little of both ...

The downside: This is happening in Amazon fulfillment centers. A law firm representing Amazon said in a letter to the National Labor Relations Board:

> "Amazon's system tracks the rates of each individual associate's productivity and automatically generates any warnings or terminations regarding quality or productivity without input from supervisors."[83]

This is where robot problems begin in HR. AI algorithms are getting smart enough to screen work candidates, hire Vucans, monitor performance, and fire under-performers with little human intervention. Welcome to work dystopia.

The upside: Robotics at the macro scale may have life changing, positive possibilities with automated highways with self-driving electric cars providing more work opportunities. Just think of how your living patterns may profoundly be altered as you live many miles away while driven to work by a robot.

Years ago as an engineer, I used rule-based programs or what were known as expert systems to codify work. My goal was to take repeatable processes that experts were using and come up with rules for replicating their knowledge and decision-making into a set of rules. Machines have gone one step further where they can discover patterns and explicitly create programming rules on their own. Machines over the last few years have been getting smarter due to their ability to learn and develop human-like abilities such as Apple's Siri program.

Work Lesson Earned: Our Future of Work is straight-forward:

> "If automation continues at its current pace, 400 million workers around the globe will be displaced by 2030. in spite of the vast economic effects of these changes will bring, will we seize the opportunity to reconceive the very meaning of work"[84]

ROBOTS ARE COMING - FOR YOUR KID'S JOB

"Are Robots Coming For Your Job? 'Eventually, Yes'."
Headline of N.Y. Times Article - September 21, 2018

So your kid wants to go to Stanford Medical School to be a radiologist or other medical specialist. Your kid spent 16 years excelling in school, then 10 years in med school, residency, specialization, and board certification. Your kid is kinda of a geek not having spent much time doing much else aside from studying. But, it was worth it. With his medical specialization, he can make a half a million dollars a year. Great career planning! Great risk-based, decision-making! Only one problem …

Machine learning and artificial intelligence are getting to the point where smart machines can read and interpret a scan from a MRI machine as well as or even better than a physician or radiologist.[85] So, now what?

The fear of work, job, and career displacement is real. New robots and bots can see better than humans. Robots can drive automobiles. Robots can conduct document reviews for litigation. Robots can automatically write articles. Robots can operate on humans. And, robots can do these as well as or even better than a Vucan. And, what will happen in five years?

So, what do we recommend your son or daughter do for a Vucan career or work? The *Future of Work* being robotic and AI driven seems dystopian and dark in terms of careers. Why? Machines are encroaching on our lives. You probably want but don't have a personal road map with guidelines and mileposts in terms of how to deal with personal work disruption.

Work Lesson Earned: The challenge is AI and robotics is breaching our Vucan boundaries of comfort and knowledge. Vucans don't know where work starts or will end with smart machines. Vucans don't know the rules of how to collaborate with these machines. Vucans don't know how to deal with the ethics and assumptions of RBPS and RBDM with robots and smart machines. The good: opportunities look great for those who can solve these problems.

WORK AS HUNGER GAMES

You can't look at the competition and say you're going to do it better. You have to look at the competition and say you're going to do it differently.
Steve Jobs – Apple Founder & Entrepreneur

The big change I've seen in the last few years is that some Vucans look at work, careers, and jobs as competition even as war. David D'Allessandro even wrote a book **Career Warfare: 10 Rules for Building a Successful Personal Brand and Fighting to Keep It**! Career warfare is kinda like Hunger Games!

It's a survival approach to work, where the hunter in olden times had to take smart risks and be constantly aware of immediate surroundings. Otherwise the stronger, bigger, and possibly even smarter predator would have the hunter for lunch. Could this be *Future of Work* where IQ (knowledge application), EQ (emotional application), and value execution reign supreme? Let's unpack this.

Almost all work from the receptionist to the CEO is knowledge and information based. You, individually or as part of a team, may create a new product, offer a unique suggestion, or provide value-added services. You have to use your best judgment, tools, methods, and knowledge in your work to create marketable value.

Since the risks of poor attitudes, low skills, and inadequate performance are too high, each Vucan is considered a self-managed professional. In an employee involved atmosphere, workers and teams have responsibility and authority to control their work and ultimately their destiny. Work accountability rests with each employee. Implicit is you use best judgment to do the right things right.

Then, there's value execution, which is a challenge for many Vucans. I've noticed that a lot of Vucan professionals are running faster these days. But, they don't seem to have direction. They confuse running for direction and speed for impact. They confuse process for outcomes. Ask them about this and their response is that they'll run faster. My thought is if you don't know where you're going, no path will take you there.

Work Lesson Earned: Here's a tip. See how your boss looks at his career or her job. Does he or she believe in career warfare? If so, what are the rules of engagement? Most importantly, do you understand the rules of engagement?

#1 FACTOR TO SUCCESS: YOUR BOSS

You need to decide what problems, what opportunities, what projects you're going to work on.
Fred L. Turner – McDonald's CEO

Your boss is the #1 factor that will make or break your work. Many of us who've been in the workplace understand this only too well.

You'll work for bosses who steal your ideas or take credit for what you've done. You'll work for 'death march' or 'my way or the highway' bosses. In other companies, you'll have 'stewardship' bosses, who don't seem to coordinate or execute well. In the middle, there are many different styles of boss, supervisor, manager, executive, or even leader.

Scott Adams, the Dilbert creator, called project work 'boss diversification.' Adams says: "the worst risk you can face is to have one boss, somebody who can make your life miserable and then decide when it is time for you to go." By diversifying (side-hustle) work, you lower the risk of working for a horrific boss. "The more customers and clients you have, the safer you are. People are going to gravitate to what's safest," he continues.[86]

Do you wonder why Vucans don't want to be a boss? In a good to great economy, the power of a bad supervisor or manager has diminished. If a Vucan offers real value, people can sell their services to the highest bidder. And, many companies, are having a harder time retaining key workers.

Project hopping is good when the economy is strong and there's a lot of demand for specialized skills that companies are willing to pay for. As a general rule, when times are tough, it's better to homestead the job and wait out the bad times.

Work Lesson Earned: One way to survive a bad boss is to have side-hustle projects. Think of this as work diversification. Eighty percent of the work in an organization may be project oriented. Organizations are projectizing their core processes. Most consulting, engineering, and medicine are already 100% projectized.

GIG-WORK

T.V.'s weird because it's both the greatest gig as an actor potentially because it can be all this work for all this time, but there are so many question marks at every stage of the process.
Caitlin Fitzgerald – Actress & Filmmaker

Work, careers, and jobs shift like quicksand. The destruction of traditional jobs, the emergence of new careers, the role of new work rules, and the fundamental disruption of work can't be ignored or dismissed. It's happening! It's real! It's scary! It's crazy.

The U.S. economy is creating millions of jobs for which there are few qualified applicants. However, many new jobs are fundamentally different from what many of us were trained or expected to do. The new jobs require tech smarts. They require value-adding capabilities. They are contingent on continued great performance. They are continuously monitored. They are often short term. All of these things challenge and contradict lifetime or even long-term employment.

The assumption of lifetime employment implied you had a stable wage that would predictably increase and if you performed well, you'd receive a bonus. Otherwise, your wages grew based on performance, attitude, and cost of living. Lifetime security and employment are myths because of marketplace changes. Free agency is coming to all professions and all Vucans.

William Bridges, a profound thinker of work, called this in **Job Shift** 'de-jobbing.' He made the critical distinction between a job and work. A job was something you did for a short time. Jobs to be filled would disappear over the long-term while work would always need to be done.

A recent study indicated that up to one-third of the companies reported using professional temporaries as managerial, professional, and technical specialists. In hi-tech companies, it's not unusual to find 40% of the workers are high-paid temps or contractors. Vucans with specialized knowledge and skills can earn a lot of money.

Work Lesson Earned: How do you feel about the concept of 'gig-work'? Are you resentful? Do you feel entitled? Are you privileged? Do you have to reimagine your work and yourself. It's important to explore these feelings and understand how they may hinder and/or promote your work, career, and job success.

FUNDAMENTAL WORK UNIT

When you look for a job, you are looking for something that is fading from the socioeconomic picture because it is past its evolutionary prime.
William Bridges – Change Author

A few years ago, *Harvard Business Review,* said the following about gig-work:

> "The fundamental unit of such an economy is not the corporation but the individual. Tasks aren't assigned and controlled through a stable chain of management but rather are carried out autonomously by independent contractors. These electronically connected freelancers – e-lancers – join together into fluid and temporary networks to produce and sell goods and services. When a job is done - after a day, a month, and a year – the network dissolves, and its members become independent agents again, circulating through the economy, seeking the next assignment."[87]

If the above quote is prescient, why should someone hire you or use your services in a crowded field of human and machine applicants? Some human competitors may be smarter and offer the same services as you do. Some machine applications may work faster and cheaper than you. And, work can be done virtually and just-in-time in any place of the world. Then, there are the robots, who may do many tasks as well as you can or better.

And, there's a chance that you may be unemployed, which would be a personal paradigm shift. You may need to change your point of view of work from risk-averse to risk-sensitive or even to risk-taking perspective. You may have to evolve and see work much like a startup sees opportunity as possibility and even probability where others see impossibility.

Another personal paradigm shift is to see your work in terms of a value exchange. Value can be designing a product or delivering an essential service. The value exchange is a difficult concept to accept for long-term employees and union members.

Work Lesson Earned: As a fundamental business unit, so what is your value-added differentiator and why should somebody hire you? This is the essence of establishing a personal brand in a disruptive economy. You need to be prepared to work in a gig and robotic economy.

DESIGNING THE BRAND YOU

It's important to build a personal brand because it's the only thing you're going to have. Your reputation online, and in the new business world is pretty much the game, so you've got to be a good person. You can't hide anything, and more importantly, you've got to be out there at some level.

Kyle Pearce – Entrepreneur

Kardashians. Donald Trump. Tim Ferriss. Sean Ogle. Barack Obama. What do they all have in common? Strong personal brands. You know who they are and what they stand for by their personal branding and even personal disruption.

Tom Peters, the management guru of **In Search of Excellence**, knew a good thing when he saw one. He picked up on the theme that we'll be self-employed professionals and came up the expression: The Brand Called You™ almost 20 years ago. Great idea and great timing! Peters said it succinctly: "We are CEOs of our own companies: Me Inc. To be in business today, our most important job is to be head marketer for The Brand Called You."[88]

Personal disruption starts with introspection. You'll have to assess your work choices and decisions before you can reengineer your career. Just as any business, you'll have to understand your core proficiencies, understand what's valued in the marketplace, and if necessary tweak your existing competencies or even develop new ones.

Millennial creatives are great in establishing virtual personas and personal brands in social media. Caroline Calloway, one of Instagram's first influencer brands, explains it this way:

> "However, as an artist and as a creative person, it's both my responsibility and my right to support myself so that I can make the things I want to make. I acknowledge that in order to do that, it behooves me to understand and respond to the ways other people might see Caroline Calloway as a brand, and to act accordingly. Even though I don't see it in my heart this way, I understand why I must in order to be the best businesswoman that I can be. I need to support myself."[89]

Work Lesson Earned: What do you need to do to develop your Brand You? Execute tasks. Finish projects on time, on budget, within scope with satisfied customers. Design killer products or apps. Have self-discipline. Be resilient. Be able to balance peaks in work activity. Make money.

SO, WHAT DO YOU COMPETE ON?

A brand for a company is like a reputation for a person. You earn reputation by trying to do hard things well.
Jeff Bezos – Founder of Amazon

"Brand is everything, and everything is brand" according to **Advertising for Humanity** founder Dan Pallotta, in a 2011 article for *Harvard Business Review*: The title pretty much says it all. So, a little back ground may provide context.

The idea of corporate branding started in the 1920s with the rise of American consumer culture. The idea behind branding was to differentiate one product from another. Personal branding is how Vucans establish and monetize personal competitiveness. The idea is to differentiate personal competencies, value-adds, and successes. Personal branding is shifting from work practices to issues of personal narrative and identity. Let's look at social media.

Social media influencers have changed personal branding. Personal branding is all about your social media, selfies, and Instagram. It's about your story on how you market yourself as a product or service to the world. It's your compelling story or narrative of where you started, how you evolved, and how you got to where you are today. It's about your struggles, what you learned, and how you applied the learnings. Think **Work Lesson Earned**.

Personal branding is global. One-name influencers. Nano-personas. Personal brand coaches. Much of the interest in social media and social platforms is based on establishing a personal brand and then scaling to a global influencer brand. And, successful social media influencers are brandpreneurs, who can make millions of dollars a year through social media.

At a work level, LinkedIn is a personal branding platform. Employers on LinkedIn can see your experience, identity, skills, abilities, strengths, and passions. They can see your work and track record to see how you overcame failure and obstacles to be who and what you are.

Work Lesson Earned: Your personal brand is your story. So if you have or had to develop a personal brand, it's critical that you know what you compete on? Or, expressed another way: What's your compelling value-add or unique selling proposition?

CRUSHING IT

If you want bling or if you want to buy the Jets (football team) - work. That's how you get it.
Gary Vee - Entrepreneur

Be Gary Vee. Be Elon Musk. So, do you want to be a founder of a tech startup or an entrepreneur? So, what does it take? The founder narrative is legendary.

The Silicon Valley nerd narrative goes like this. You live a monastic life. Your work is your life. You never take a vacation. You seldom date. You never watch TV. You're the gamer with world class twitch. You're the crack developer. You're the startup bro. You're the girl boss. And, you rule the world. And like all narratives, there are some truth to it. Look at techies like Jobs, Sandberg, Musk, Ma, Reid, etc.

Or look at non-techies like Gary Vaynerchuk. Gary Vee is the complete achievement celebrity. Gary Vee evangelizes a mono-maniacal or single focused view of work and success. He's a judge on the Planet of Apps, where app developers compete for funding to develop the killer app. He's a media celeb.

New hustle hard gurus have sprung up in almost every country in this world. Hundreds of YouTubers follow their achievements. Hustler is a term of endearment and achievement. The goal of a hustler is to be a maker, do'er, founder, girl leader, and worker for the bling.

An entire industry has sprung up with an internet driven message of the prosperity gospel of work. Start your own company and make a killing. In some ways, this is the dream. Others say, it's the aspirational vision of Millennial and Gen Z generations.

Work Lesson Earned: Check out the 'Crushing It' books for bro's and girl's. They focus on risk-taking and innovation. These books focus on finding a personal competitive advantage to differentiate your personal abilities and skills. These books cross cultures. Gary Vee's 'Crushing It' sounds over the top for much of the West. However, ask Asians what they think? This is their normal as they're trained to excel. They epitomize 18 hour work days, monomaniacal focus and achievement. Could this be the basis for today's fear and anxiety?

HUSTLE CULTURE

Your personal brand is a promise to your clients... a promise of quality, consistency, competency, and reliability.
Jason Hartman – Singer & Song Writer

Startups are the new vision and mission for Vucans almost regardless of age. Startups offer the dream of working long hours, creating, being your own boss, making money on your terms, and changing the world. This is the ultimate dream in self-management.

A new genre of gurus urge Vucans to postpone or even forgo an education to do startups. Peter Thiel, the co-founder of PayPal and Palantir, is the no-education leader. Thiel offers a fellowship to young founders who want to do and make a difference. The kicker of the Fellowship is that a Vucan has to skip or quit college to work with Thiel's network of founders, investors, and engineers. Thiel Fellowship "gives $100K to young people who want to build new things instead of sitting in a classroom."[90]

The Silicon Valley attitude is to ideate, learn, apply, test, and do again until you succeed. This is counter intuitive in many parts of the world that shames or demonizes failure. The startup movement way is to try new things, test them, and fail fast through incremental exploration.

Think hustle RBPS and RBDM. The idea is you can limit the damage by placing small bets on opportunities, where you think there's incremental or even substantial upside thus limiting the consequences of downside risk and failure. So the idea is not to bet the company but develop marketable ideas that can be replicated, scaled, and monetized. Through these little hits, you gain insight into how to ideate a profitable venture.

Work Lesson Earned: In hustle culture, Vucans must be flexible, entrepreneurial, agile, and lean. Hustle Vucans are focused on being their own bosses and making a difference. Vucans use RBPS and RBDM to self-manage. They focus on smart opportunities, take intelligent risks, and use disruption to their advantage. They want to design their glass and fill it with their choice of beverage or weed (in states where it's legal).

HOW TO ENHANCE BRAND YOU

If you are not a brand, you are a commodity.
Robert Kiyosaki – Rich Dad Author

As the marketplace, customers, and companies disrupt, what communicates core values or a sense of who you are? Once you know this, how can you enhance the Brand You and your reputational equity. Let's look at your personal attributes.

A personal brand tells Vucans who you are, what you can do, and what they can count on from you. It's part of your character and personality. Can you be a recognizable brand? You bet. That's what social media and influencing is all about. It's a matter of creating personal buzz and interest. This may mean managing signature projects, vlogging, clever meming, writing best-selling books, influencing, or talking at professional meetings. With social media, it's easier than ever to create personal buzz.

There are many studies that identify the attributes of product success. What makes a product a success can make you successful. Once a customer or stakeholder is identified, then you can enhance your worth or value by:

- Finding new ways to solve a problem, scratch an itch, or reduce a pain.
- Developing abilities not available from competitors.
- Providing good or higher value for money.
- Finding a better way of meeting customer requirements and needs.
- Providing excellent quality relative to competitor's products.
- Offering better price performance characteristics than a competitor's products or services.

Work Lesson Earned: I 'got it' about personal branding and influencing when Martha Stewart, a convicted felon, continued to brand herself as the 'Taste Goddess.' When she was incarcerated, I thought she was toast. When released, she rebranded into 'Taste Maven' again. Social media influencers with millions of followers can pivot on a dime and quickly reestablish authenticity with their large audience. Influencers have the power of personal branding to have Vucans buy things. Influencers write books, build apps, and vlog. Why not you?

YOUR LEAN STARTUP

As you consider building your own minimum viable product, let this simple rule suffice: remove any feature, process, or effort that does not contribute directly to the learning you seek.
Eric Ries – Lean Startup Author

Eric Ries is the author of the **Lean Startup**. The idea of the **Lean Startup** is to start small, test for success, tweak the business model, replicate the model, and scale. Sounds easy. But, really hard to do successfully.

The idea is to try out your business idea and fail fast in testing the idea. If an idea works with a prototype tested against real customers, this can be the beginning of a successful business model. If the idea works then the product is brought to market. If the idea doesn't work, you pivot and the process starts again with a new model, product, service, or prototype.

Startup world is not for the faint of heart. A startup has a lot of moving parts: Customers x Sales x Operations x Marketing x Engineering x Fulfillment x Investors x Magic x Self-Management = Success. Remember basic algebra – if any of these factors becomes 0, result is you failed. Do the math, there are n key success factors and $2^n - 1$ ways to fail and only 1 way to succeed. In our previous equation, there are 9 success factors so there are 1,999,999,999 (almost 2 billion to the math challenged) ways to fail and 1 way to succeed.[91]

So, what area should you do a startup. **Tip:** choose carefully. For example, tech startup land is full of testosterone. It's not inclusive or diverse. Asian male Vucans excel at math and coding. The monoculture of nerdism is global.

Is the startup work ethic good or bad? Is work a means to an end, such as fame or money? It may be for some if not many. And that's okay. This group of Vucans understand where they're going and what they have to do to get there.

Work Lesson Earned: Why is the hustling it or 996 work ethic necessary? It's a matter of numbers. Most products, startups, retailers fail. The numbers are stunning as up to 90% of small businesses fail. The critical issue is whether the founders learn from failure and have the grit to try again.

STARTUP LIFE MANTRA

If you cannot fail, you cannot learn.
Eric Ries - Author

Silicon Valley is dream land - the place where dreams are made. The dream of making billions, not millions The dream of being with one's tribe. The dream of thinking, creating, and doing different.

But as you know, nothing comes free. There's no free lunch. A great idea executed effectively can't guarantee instant success. This is done through hustle, grind, grit, and crushing it. Just look at the U.S. women's soccer team. However, this path is not for everyone.

My story: My life's mantra is: "be a risk taker, fail fast, and fall forward ." I'm an engineer, who takes risks, that means that I fail 90% of the time. Not good. How do I survive? Grit is required. Resilience ensures that I get back to task after lots of blood, sweat, and tears. It's not a fun ride. But like crack, risk-taking is addictive.

So, is there a well-defined success path? No. If there were, everyone would follow it and there would be no risk. So, it's different for everyone. The startup mantra is a personal blueprint of risk-taking by following and applying your lessons earned. But remember, they have to be applied based on context.

For many, the startup life is a rite of passage to corporate and individual business success. Companies want to self-disrupt and act like a startup. So, startup life lessons learned evolve into work lessons earned that can be used in lots of businesses and work opportunities. Startup life is built on trials, errors, and numerous failures. This is never fun! None of us like to admit failure. Many of us have been taught to deny failure. Many of us react to failure and self-defeating ways. However it is a requirement for business and entrepreneurship.

Work Lesson Earned: However, doing work lessons earned and applying them requires a mental and behavioral shift that frankly is difficult. It takes a certain talent to embrace and even acknowledge failure. In some cultures, failure is not an option.

DILBERT'S BRAND DIFFERENTIATION

The American Dream is still alive out there, and hard work will get you there. You don't necessarily need to have an Ivy League education or to have millions of dollars startup money. It can be done with an idea, hard work and determination.
Bill Rancic – Entrepreneur

A common theme in **Working It** is there are fewer great paying jobs and many more aspirants with non-marketable college educations and high loans. Some call this career warfare for the best paying jobs. Some call this a crisis of privilege.

So, what can you do to compete if you're average like most of us? Gordon Scott Adams, the creator of the cartoon **Dilbert**, believes the future for many Vucans will be some startup, craft, creativity, small business, or entrepreneurship. He offers these reality based, tongue-in-cheek tips for success:

> "Combine your creativity in unexpected ways. For example you may be an average student in four or five areas. However when you combine these four or five unusual skills, you may find that the combination of all these skills create something that is truly differentiating and world class."

There's a lot of wisdom in Adams's advice. In my hometown, business heroes are coders, curators, creatives, founders, and makers in nichey areas. These Vucans are Millennial's and boomers who start small businesses. They share common interests such as believing in fairness, diversity, and self-actualization. They believe in working in the Green Work World. Or, they simply want to keep busy and make a little money on the side.

Work Lesson Earned: RBPS, RBDM, and grit can overcome lack of privilege. Starting a company is a form of self-expression for a maker, curator, and hustler. It's easier than ever with lower barriers of entry. It's easier to be successful. A Vucan with a four-month cyber or big data online certificate may make more than a Vucan who invested a hundred thousand dollars in a non-marketable degree.

STARTUP WORK: BEST OF TIMES. WORST OF TIMES

If you're not paying for it, you're not the customer; you're the product being sold.
Tim O'Reilly CEO O'Reilly

The other day I was watching Dickens's **Tale of Two Cities** movie. I was really stunned how it reflects the life of a startup. It's been a while since you read it in high school, so here's the start of the novel:

> "It was the best of times, it was the worst of times, it was the age of wisdom, it was the age of foolishness, it was the epoch of belief, it was the epoch of incredulity, it was the season of light, it was the season of darkness, it was the spring of hope, it was the winter of despair..."[92]

The above quote distills startup life and work. Many who have thrived, survived, or failed in a startup say that it's the 'best and worst of times' they've had in their work lives.

Let's unpack the above quote in terms of a typical startup:

- **Startup work** is the best of times as you have the passion, vision, and dream to do something that can change the world or make a difference or make a lot of money. All these are OK. These are the things that drive a Vucan to excel, dream, or do something different. Your personal dream results in something special for you – think and do something almost supernatural with mono-maniacal focus and energy.
- **Startup work** is the worst of times since it can drain physical, spiritual, family, friends, and relationships. This is coupled with paranoia, fear, and anxieties – the personal disruptions that startup work can entail.
- **Startup work** is the age of ideas and wisdom because you try to do things that have not been thought of or done before. You're on top of your game. You're invincible. High-fives all around.

- **Startup work** is the age of foolishness because you feel indestructible along with the startup team's echo chamber. You're all saying the same things to each other. You're believers. You don't listen to mentors, apostates, and naysayers even VC's on your board.

- **Startup work** is the epoch of belief because they feel, believe, and think that you're at the center of creation, competitiveness, and innovation, which may be London, Berlin, San Francisco, Seattle, Tokyo, or Shanghai. All of you are drinking the same Kool-Aid.

- **Startup work** is the epoch of incredulity since the team believes all mountains can be scaled, problems can be solved, obstacles can be removed, and nothing stands in the way of world domination.

- **Startup work** believes it's the season of light since the team has been chosen by the geek gods to innovate and VC's to create world changing apps.

- **Startup work** is the season of darkness since new obstacles rise up daily. The highs and lows result in high amplitude, sinusoidal, emotional curves.

- **Startup work** is the season of hope as one problem after another is solved and hard decisions are made.

- **Startup work** is the winter of despair when after many 100-hour weeks for a year, the project is finished or app is developed. One problem: there's no demand for the product. Lots of questions: What went wrong? Were assumptions wrong. Why did the design suck? What decisions should have been made differently? Are they fixable? So, what now? Pivot? Countless other justify cations and recriminations.

Work Lesson Earned. So, make sure you're working on the right problem. Make sure there's demand for your solution. Make sure Vucans want it and will pay for it. Remember: You're not a philanthropy. It's all about the money!

SMALL BUSINESS FUTURE OF WORK

The largest employer in the U.S. and in most countries is small businesses. Small business is hard. Hours are long. Profit margins are slim. And, governments most of the time don't look out for their interests of the small business owner. Big problem for startups and side-hustlers.

Small businesses throughout the world generate new or net jobs. The challenge is that most small businesses are disrupted in ways that no one ever expected.

Small businesses in 2020 will be focusing on making a profit. Why? In most countries, it's getting tougher to make a profit. A small business, considered less than 500 people, is squeezed by rising wages, trade war tariffs, and increasing cost of goods. They often can't pass additional costs to the customer.

There's also the Amazon effect. Vucans are buying online. Each country and each sector has an Amazon equivalent. These online shopping centers remove the middle distribution company and retailers. The online shops can sell products cheaper and often pay for shipping.

Then in many western countries, there are increasing minimum wage requirements. In the U.S., there's a push for $15 dollar an hour minimum wage or what's called a living wage. This of course is different in many countries. However, the trend is similar. These small business and startup challenges will impact many workers.

Work Lesson Earned: Small business is often a family or retail business. They want to do the right things. The reality is most small businesses fail. They suffer from lots of regulation. Their margins are razor thin. Many owners and startup founders make less than the minimum wage.

So, why hire and pay Vucans for making more than the owners? And, small business can't afford employees with mandatory health benefits. The middle class in many countries often small business owners is disappearing.

MILLENNIAL VUCAN CHALLENGES

Don't lament so much about how your career is going to turn out. You don't have a career. You have a life. Do the work. Keep the faith.
Cheryl Strayed - Writer

Vucan workers around the world are angry and resisting. I live and work in Portland Oregon. Portland is the epicenter of Gen Z and Millennial angst and Antifa in the U.S. I've seen the anger and experienced the resentment first hand from Millennials (30 year old's) and Gen Z'ers (20 year old's). It comes from their dashed dreams, lost opportunities, and financial indenture to student loans.

Millennials and Gen Z'ers want to design their own work rules, which may be different than what management, company culture, stakeholders, and investors want. I would say that 70 to 80% of Millennials don't like or want to follow today's competitive and disruptive work rules.

While these generations are not homogeneous, they face common challenges. College loans. Financial collapse. Disenfranchised. Unmet expectations. Angst. Life and work struggles.

The below quote from *Gen Z Insights* captures Millennial angst:

> "In 2018, I've felt growing pressure to compete for a spot in the world. I've had to change my mindset from skating through life and school to applying myself to get a job and work towards college. I realized I need to stand out more than my parents and grandparents did, because the competition has become fiercer to get into good schools and to find a high-paying job. The pressure I've felt over the past year has made me change my outlook on life and take a hard look at what I want my future to be."[93]

Work Lesson Earned: Studies point to the ability to be resilient and comfortable with VUCA may be tied to happiness, higher earnings, and better performance.[94] Gen Z and Millennial workers throughout the world are the original Vucans. Workers from 18 to 37 are twice as likely to be uncomfortable with VUCA. Dictionary.com says "the world Gen Z has inherited is one of unprecedented chaos."[95] They are the new precariat.

VUCAN MANAGEMENT CHALLENGES

You now have to decide what 'image' you want for your brand. Image means personality. Products, like people, have personalities, and they can make or break them in the market place.

David Ogilvy – Marketing Guru

Many executives I know are frankly scared these days. Competitive and business rules have been disrupted too quickly. They don't understand their competitive landscape and its new rules of engagement. Why? There's too much VUCA due to offshore competition, digital disruption, automation, robotics, and artificial intelligence. They can't forecast based on historical, stable, and straight-line assumptions.

Executives need to generate revenue and cut costs. In the next few years, you'll see head-count reductions due to automation. But when the company is cutting to the bone, innovation seems to be lost as a way to generate new sources of revenue. Companies find it harder to innovate constantly and lean rapidly to sustain profitability.

Executives face the challenge that the history of recent tech and startups is full of neat ideas that just didn't cut it. The customer had unrealistic expectations. The development team was clueless of what the customer really wanted. The tech-turkey app, product, or service simply didn't connect with the end user.

And, there are time and cost pressures. Companies develop a new generation of products yearly or even quarterly. Competition is Darwinian. Although more than 13,000 new products hit the market each year, fewer than 40% will be around a few years later. The time-to-market math and political climate such as continuous trade wars make work decisions difficult.

Work Lesson Earned: If you're innovative and have experience commercializing products, then you'll be well positioned over the next 5 years. If you're fundamentally not innovative, then find ways to support innovation, commercialize it, or monetize it. As much as possible, you want to be on the innovation and revenue side of equation, not the expense side.

WHEN SHOULD YOU SELF-DISRUPT?

When you make the decision to start something new, first figure out the jobs you want to do. Then position yourself to play where no one else is playing.
Whitney Johnson - Writer

When should you self-disrupt? There's no easy answer. However, it's about risk.

Do you know your personal value proposition?   If you don't, sooner than later you'll have a work wake up call. Your abilities, career direction, or work are not aligned with your employer's business strategies or customer's market requirements. You may have less authority, new boss, new position, marginal performance review, or even a job loss. Your employer has a new business model. Your employer changed its business rules. Your employer may want to outsource. Your employer may see employees as an expense, not an asset. Your employer may see workers and contractors as expendable. These result in stress.

Each of these is a stimulus to examine what you do right, what you could do better, what you could learn, and what you should do different. Your goal is to conduct an honest career gap analysis and self-disrupt. This is work because you may have to stare at the mirror and conduct an objective analysis. I call this the 'career ledger sheet.' What are your work, job, and career assets and liabilities? You want to enhance your assets and minimize your liabilities. It isn't an easy process to assume new roles, establish new relationships, establish new directions, offer new ideas, be proactive, learn new behaviors, or work effectively. This requires time, effort, resources, and resiliency. All of which take time away from other activities. But, it's your life and work resiliency!

Mary Lynn Pulley in **Losing Your Job – Reclaiming Your Soul** called the ability to bounce back from adversity, 'work resilience.' You have an inner life force to bounce back and carry on. You become resilient by developing and nourishing positive relationships. You may reach the stage in your career when options are fewer, career choices are limited and you don't know where to go or what to do. This is a time for reflection, for repositioning yourself if necessary and for learning resilience.[96]

Work Lesson Earned: Address these important work questions: Where are you going? How are you going to get there? Will the journey or the destination make you happy? What are the tradeoffs along the way? Are you willing to make the required sacrifices? What do you need to learn to get where you want?

SELF-MANAGEMENT - YOUR NEXT STEPS

- What do you think the rules for engagement with a smart machine should be?
- Do you believe machines may or will replace humans by mechanizing and automating work?
- Can a machine take your job and replace you?
- How can the machine help you work efficiently, effectively, and economically?
- How do you think you can work with a machine to augment, supplement, or complement your decision-making and problem-solving?
- Alternatively, are you offended by the above ideas? And if you are in what ways?
- Can a career, even yours perhaps, be managed like a product brand?
- What has been your career and work-lifecycle?
- What products or services have you developed or significantly participated in developing or delivering in the last:
    - Month?
    - 6 months?
    - 1 year?
- How is your value measured?
- Who values your contributions and how are they recognized?
- How would you personally brand yourself, specifically what would you do?
- What is your key product or service value contributor?
- What is your product or service's core differentiator?
- Do you offer any 'wow' factors?
- What is your personal brand promise?
- How do you personally innovate?
- Do you deliver on your promises?
- What do you love to do?
- Do you do what you love?

PROCESSES

-

CORE WORK

In this 7P's section, we discuss the core Process paradigm. Process work means different things depending on context. Process work for big companies involves core work processes that are repetitive, continuous, and controlled. Process work involves developing new business models – new ways to solve a problem, add value, make a decision, and innovate a service. For example, Amazon's core ability is to reinvent itself through new business models. Amazon started with books and then went into adjacent segments reinventing new ways to discover and capture value through automation and facilitating online business from one segment to another.

Core processes are the first work to be automated. Automation through AI or machine learning are paradigm busters. For example, automation has disrupted the retail work business model. Let's look at it. Retail workers are supposed to help customers. Forget customer experience, think user experience (UX). Automation puts users to work in 'no or few worker' retail environments. Look at the 'selfs' next time you're shopping for food. Self-food selection. Self-service. Self-check out. Self-bagging. Self-pay. Self-security. Any way you get the idea. Automation has arrived and is disrupting food retail.

VUCAN DRIVERS - PROCESSES

Old School	New School
Core process work	Project work
Fixed organizational structure	Fluid & agile structure
Offshoring	Near shoring
Buy in 'Make or Buy'	Make in 'Make or Buy'
Outsourcing to China	Outsource to other Asian countries
Chinese partnering and collaboration	Digital Curtain with China
Made in China	Made in U.S.
Transactional sourcing	Enterprise focused sourcing
Vertical organization and integration	Flexible organizational models
Static business model	Agile business models
Buy products offshore	Make products internally
Industrial and factory automation	Automation everywhere
Ownership economy	Sharing economy
Brick and mortar business model	Online business model
Telephone and voice economy	App economy
Regular apps	Super apps
Hard skills	Soft & hard skills
Mega-influences	Micro-influencers
Specialist	Multi-skilled
Work commitment	Work-life balance

PROCESSES @ RISK

Process is a particular course of action intended to achieve a result.
Dictionary

Processes are how work is done in many companies. The traditional process structure was a pyramid with the Chief Executive Officer at the top. Work flowed down and across the organization. Technology, new business models, globalization, customer's expectations, automation have created new business models and work processes:

- **Organism.** The organic organization is a current hot idea. Michael Rothschild in **Bionomics: Economy as Ecosystem** describes organizations, industries, teams, and even Gaia earth as organisms. The internet is an example of an organic organization. What characterizes these organizational organisms? The organism merges, melds, and morphs to fit external requirements.
- **Federalist structure.** Federalist describes a structure of separate companies or individuals loosely clustered into an informal collaboration. The companies are grouped and matrixed around businesses, products functions, regions, type, software, or customers instead of the hierarchal pyramid.
- **Core process.** A common business wisdom is to focus on core processes and competencies or in other words, stick to your knitting. In this way, key process team and individual skills are developed that differentiate one company from another. Large companies and startups follow this model so they can replicate and scale.
- **Project work.** Lean startups and companies are organized around tasks and projects. Highly focused teams do a specific job and when the project is finished, the team disbands.
- **Ever changing organization.** Traditional or Newtonian business model doesn't fit well in VUCA time. Organizations don't have time to react to reestablish stability. The stable state is evolving to the current norm - the VUCA organization that goes through continual digital transformations.

Work Lesson Earned: Is there one best structure? Companies and startups are trying to figure out what's the best work structure in VUCA time. Probably not. A flexible, lean structure satisfies stakeholders using the fewest resources.

PROCESS RULES

If your goals are ambitious and crazy enough, even failure will be a pretty good achievement.
Laszlo Bock – Author

Work and process rules are guidelines, tips and tools that can lead to success. Thomas Davenport, author **of Thinking for a Living** said:

> "To treat something as a process is to impose a formal structure on it – to identify its beginning, end, and intermediate steps, to clarify who the customer is for it, to measure it, to take stock of how well it is currently being performed, and ultimately to improve it."[97]

How are process work rules developed? When I started working, I thought most work rules were defined in policies, procedures, and work instructions. Was I wrong? In reality, these manuals were often used as a doorstop. Much of work consists process, functional, and implicit rules.

- Process rules are how work gets done in a company. Process rules outline the flow of work, resources, ideas, monies, and other mission critical assets. Process rules are usually horizontal cutting across vertical silos.
- Functional rules are the rules of the work silos of the organization. These rules can be functional, service, or location based. For example, engineering, accounting, and finance are each a vertical that may have its own rules.
- Implicit rules are the unwritten rules of work. They can be as common sensical as, demonstrating good etiquette and politeness at work. The list of implicit rules is vast and unknowable unless shared. As well, implicit rules can change from employer to employer and from function to function even within an organization.

Work Lesson Earned: Discover the underlying processes to your work, career, and job. The current world of work has mushy and ambiguous rules. To work and be successful today, it's critical to know the real and implicit work rules. A few rules are prescriptive and others are implicit. As much as possible, try to decipher and learn them. If you're new to the organization, find a mentor. Ask questions of your work and career. It's critical if you want to be successful and happy.

CORE PROCESS RULES

What you want to do is innovate on your product and your business model, management structure is not where I would try to innovate.
Sam Altman – Programmer and Investor

All companies, even global corporations, have discovered they can't be all things to all Vucans. As companies attempted to please different customers with a large variety of products, problems arose. Resources were spread too thin so a company could only do certain things moderately well. The wise decision was to focus and develop 'world class', core process competencies. There's a good business reason for this.

Process orientation involves a change of mindset, a personal disruption in how you perceive and approach work. A process orientation is a paradigm shift away from the functional and hierarchal to a horizontal model of business. A process orientation involves these interrelated factors:

- **Structure.** A core process is smooth, balanced, structured, seamless, value-adding, replicable, efficient, effective, and economic. The process has a beginning and an end. It consists of a number of value-adding steps, each of which has a customer and a supplier.
- **Layout.** A process orientation is a horizontal, end-to-end view of work. A process may cut across an organization into the supplier base and even to the final customer. A process can span different functions, plants, and departments throughout the organization. Process orientation seems to work well in matrixed organizations.
- **Accountability.** A project team or self-managed individual is responsible for a process step or even for the entire process from beginning to end. In process language, this accountability is called process ownership and self-management.

Work Lesson Earned: The closer an employee or manager is to the core, the easier it's to demonstrate long-term value. But, closer to the core means that functions will be the first to be automated.

HANDY'S WORK MODEL

Every single industry is going through a major business model and technology oriented disruption.

Aaron Levie - Entrepreneur

Charles Handy, probably the smartest workplace guru, said thirty years ago that work is fundamentally changing. Companies own core intellectual assets including proprietary processes and intellectual property.

Handy then coined the notion of ½ by 2 by 3 rule of corporate fitness. This workplace is characterized by half as many Vucans on the payroll, paid twice as much, producing three times as much. Handy's work model consists of 3 concentric circles:

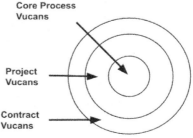

- **Inner ring.** The inner ring, the organizational core, is composed of corporate insiders, functional managers, and core Vucans. The inner ring workers are usually full time equivalent employees. They have full benefits, salaries, retirements, and vacations. They are the glue that holds the organization together and grows it. They generate new ideas, innovative products, and add corporate value.
- **Middle ring.** Portfolio or project Vucans inhabit the middle ring according to Handy. These Vucans are contractors, gig-workers, or temporary workers. Vucans offer marketable, transferable skills, knowledge, and abilities that add organizational value. These skills are portable and can be sold to the highest bidder. A Vucan becomes an itinerant professional selling his or her skills from employer to employer. In the next section of the book, we focus on the middle ring, project workers.
- **Outer ring.** The outer ring is composed of interchangeable and disposable contract Vucans. These Vucans are less skilled, service workers. Many are marginal workers who service the repetitive needs of the organization such as food service, administrative chores, or travel services. They're paid considerably less than core and project Vucans.

Work Lesson Earned: The Handy model is a process model of work. It's critical to know if you are core, project or interchangeable employee. Many Vucans want to be process workers. However, the inner ring is at risk of disruption.

THE BLEAKNESS OF HANDY MODEL!

If you can't describe what you are doing as a process, you don't know what you're doing.
W. Edwards Deming - Quality Guru

I've introduced the Handy Work Model to thousands of Vucans in workshops and seminars. The common refrain I hear is: 'it's so bleak and negative'.

Good point. It is what it is. This is what's happening in the competitive and disrupted workplace.

When Handy first proposed his bleak vision of the corporate workplace thirty years ago, it was considered too radical. Middle managers were considered in-dispensable. Quality, information systems, accounting, training, IT, engineering, and human resource professionals were considered necessary to sustain the or-ganization. But, things disrupted, many core functions moved to the middle ring and were considered outsourceable.

Many middle management functions were downloaded to first level supervision and self-managed teams. Managerial and technical professionals became part of Handy's middle ring and were retained as long as they added value, otherwise the functions were downsized and the services outsourced to middle or outer ring workers.

The middle ring continues to evolve. Middle ring Vucans work on special pro-jects that complement or supplement the organization's core processes. For ex-ample, a company may want to develop a complex new product. The company doesn't have the resources internally so it'll hire suppliers or contractors to com-plement its existing core team with specialized skills. Or, if a fast-food restaurant anticipates a spring or summer rush of business, it'll hire temps to ensure there are sufficient Vucans to prepare food and service customers.

Work Lesson Earned: Handy model is one of the prevalent work models that companies throughout the world are adopting. Do I like it? Not really! How-ever, it makes business sense, not particularly people sense. Live with it! Figure out how to adapt and add value within the model.

HANDY WORK MODEL STORIES

You can see the Handy Work Model in many companies including Uber, Google and many highly-valued companies. Many companies use the Handy work model, which looks like this:

> "In 2015 Uber, the world's largest taxi company owns no vehicles. Facebook, the world's most popular media owner, creates no content. Alibaba, the most valuable retailer, has no inventory. And Airbnb, the world's largest accommodation provider, owns no real estate."[98]

The middle and outer rings of Google's work model look like this:

> "They (project workers) write code, handle sales calls, recruit staff, screen YouTube videos, test self-driving cars, and even manage entire teams - a sea of skilled laborers that fuel the $795 billion company but reap few of the benefits and opportunities available to direct employees .... Other companies, such as Apple Inc. and Facebook Inc., some of the most cash-rich public companies, rely on a steady influx of contractors (middle ring of Handy model).

> Investors watch employee headcount closely at these tech powerhouses, expecting that they keep posting impressive gains by maintaining skinnier workforces than older corporate titans. Hiring contractors keeps the official headcount low, and frees up millions of dollars to retain superstars in fields like artificial intelligence. The result is an invisible workforce, off the company payrolls, that does the grunt work for the Silicon Valley giants with few of the rewards."[99]

Work Lesson Earned: The big challenge to the Handy Work Model is that automation is shrinking the core further:

> "Automation is splitting the American labor force into two worlds. There's a small island of highly educated professionals making good wages at corporations like Intel or Boeing, which reap hundreds of thousands of dollars in profit per employee. That island sits in the middle of a sea of less educated workers who are stuck at businesses like hotels, restaurants and nursing homes that generate much smaller profits per employee and stay viable primarily by keeping wages low."[100]

INNER RING AUTOMATION

What is happening with automation and globalization, that's not going away.
Campbell Brown – TV News Reporter & Entrepreneur

Handy's inner ring is going through changes. Process work is reconfigured by tech, Including robotics, artificial intelligence, Internet of Things, 3-D printing, and software. Process work that can be standardized is automated as machines are getting smarter and faster.

In the last few years, artificial intelligence has the ability to understand and communicate to Vucans based upon context. For example, much of this book was dictated through the voice recognition program on a Mac computer. The rise of the machines can partially be explained because they make business sense. Vucans get angry, distracted by cell phones, attend meetings, get hungry, take breaks, and get irritated by bosses and coworkers. Machines don't.

So, what about Vucans? Many assume that jobs will fundamentally disappear. In some cases, this is true. In other cases, the jobs and work will morph into a collaboration of worker plus machine working better and faster. This is called cobot work involving machine and human. Cobots automating repetitive work and Vucans using human judgment will jointly prove to be more productive.

The challenge is to determine what jobs, functions, occupations, or work will be automated in the near future. Automation over the next five years will probably be applied to routine tasks and big data searches. Routine tasks will follow proceduralized set of activities usually defined by a clear set of rules. For example pattern recognition will be used in manufacturing to determine the quality of products. Pattern recognition will be used to identify faces and people. Pattern recognition will be used to find unexpected business opportunities in big data searches.

Work Lesson Earned: What is the role of a human worker in an automated or roboticized economy? Huge question. There are no easy answers!

FIRST JOBS TO BE AUTOMATED

You're either the one that creates the automation or you're getting automated.

Tom Preston – Werner – Software Developer

Is your job safe? McKinsey, the global consulting firm, stated that:

> "Fewer than 5% of occupations can be entirely automated using current technology. However, about 60% of all occupations could have 30% or more of their constituent activities automated. In other words, automation is likely to change the vast majority of occupations - at least to some degree - which will necessitate significant job redefinition and a transformation of business processes."[101]

McKinsey looked at the technical feasibility of automating the following seven occupations:

Occupation	Examples	Percentage Automatable
Physical work and predictable environments	Manufacturing, Food service	78%
Processing data	Finance	69%
Data collection	Transportation	64%
Physical work and unpredictable environments	Construction, Agriculture	25%
Stakeholder interactions	Retail, Finance	20%
Expertise, decision-making, creative tasks,	Professional, Education	18%
Managing others	Management	9%

Work Lesson Earned: The other day I was giving a *Future of Work* talk. I asked my tech audience how many Vucans thought their jobs would be automated or at least disrupted within five years. There were a lot of bemused looks. I thought I'd get snarky comments. Half of the audience raised their hands. I don't think anyone had been as blunt to them as I. However, they got it. It's not a matter of if, it's just a matter of when.

OUTSOURCING AND THE DIGITAL CURTAIN

China is changing Handy's work model. The middle ring includes suppliers providing products and contractors providing services. Over the years, many companies outsourced in China. This may grind to a halt over the next few years as trade war and tariffs increase. China's Digital Curtain is replacing the Soviet Union's Iron Curtain.

The Handy work model logic goes like this: If a company has core capabilities and competencies (inner ring) then it would make the product. If it does not, then it buys (middle ring) the product from 'world class' suppliers in China with complementary core process competencies.

The 'make or buy' decision is 'Do we have the expertise to manufacture a quality product and deliver it at a competitive cost?' Since many industrial tasks cannot be effectively accomplished in-house because of lack of equipment, trained personnel, or material, the answer to the question is often 'no.' This 'make or buy' decision is complicated due to Chinese price increases, IP theft, and Chinese politics. The 'make or buy' decision matters because it determines the level of investment the business will make internally as well as with suppliers. If the decision is made to outsource and offshore, work and jobs go to the offshore supplier.

Let's look at a few 'make or buy' examples: In general, high tech companies such as Intel and Microsoft competitively position themselves based on their core competencies so internal development ('make' decision) provides the most competitive advantage. In areas away from their chip design and software development, they outsource, license, or purchase required competencies.

On the other hand, Gucci sells expensive products, such as multi-thousand dollar handbags and leather goods. Gucci decided to expand its internal capabilities and competencies to assure its quality reputation through internal design, manufacturing, and distribution. It's revamping and redesigning its supply chain model to make products internally and to integrate vertically.[59]

Work Lesson Earned: Outsourcing calculus is changing due to continuous trade wars. How are you impacted? Do you work for a company whose products and services are obsolescent or can be outsourced? Do you offer professional services that can be outsourced or offshored? If 'yes' to either question, what's hindering the company from outsourcing your job? Do you see this challenge as a risk opportunity (upside risk) or a threat (downside risk)?

MADE IN 'YOUR COUNTRY'

Not only must we fight to end disastrous unfettered free trade agreements with China, Mexico, and other low wage countries, we must fight to fundamentally rewrite our trade agreements so that American products, not jobs, are our number one export.
Bernie Sanders – Politician

Many companies have this business model: develop their brand; design product (s); outsource manufacturing; test products; and sell products. Up to the 80 to 90% of the manufacturing dollar and work is sent to suppliers.

The logic for outsourcing and offshoring goes like this. The company is in the business of making widgets so why should it spend time running its own fiber optic cable, IT department, or training organization. The company wants to spend its time on things that will make a real difference to the bottom line, add value, and leverage its core competencies.

A few years ago, every company considered outsourcing non-core and even core activities. The key question was: 'Should the company outsource to China or some country in Asia because of cost competitiveness and high quality'. This applied to widgets and professional services. Even high value-added services, such as architectural, medical and other professional services was procured offshore. Companies would go to extremes. One virtual computer company hired contractors to design and build all its computers, answer repair questions, invoice bills, and ship products. The only thing it did was sell its products and maintain its remaining core competency – its brand.

A few years ago, it was source offshore, especially to China. Now, we're seeing protectionism, tariffs, domestic sourcing, insourcing (core expansion), new competitive rules, and new business models. The 'make or buy' and off-shoring decision is now changing in many companies and even countries. Every country in the world is asking the 'make or buy' question. We have 'Made in China', 'Made in India', and 'Made in Great Britain'. Why? It's all about local work and jobs.

Work Lesson Earned: Globalization, outsourcing, and off shoring are realities. The questions and concessions asked of workers and suppliers are incredible and tough. Do you know your company's 'make or buy' philosophy?

ON DEMAND WORK MODELS - SHARING THINGS

The gig economy today is not a choice of wanting to be a 1099 worker. It's work on top of other employment.
Fred Goff - CEO Jobcase.

Excessive and conspicuous consumption have been the expectation and norm in many western economies. We believed buying lots of unneeded stuff based on compulsion would make us happy, but resulted in a lot idle stuff or wasteful overcapacity. Global compulsive consumption is nearing its limits and giving rise to the sharing economy. This is called de-growth.

The sharing economy is also called the collaborative, subscription, peer-to-peer, or sharing. And, it's grown exponentially. Take a look at auto, tool, and even clothes sharing. Auto sharing companies such as Uber and Lyft were unknown ten years ago. They now have capitalizations of $120 billion for Uber and $20 billion for Lyft. Look at Airbnb the room sharing company. By the way, Uber and Lyft have never made money. And, they are everywhere.

If you want a logo design or a house cleaned, there's an app for that. The apps allow a customer and supplier to come together, negotiate the scope of work, and decide on a flat fee for doing the work. Fast, simple, and direct buyer-seller relationships, that are often off the books.

Sharing economy is also changing work. The online platforms such as Uber have displaced taxi companies throughout the world. And, disruptees are not going down without a fight. Taxi companies are organizing strikes, filing lawsuits, and leaning on regulators for protection.

And, this foreshadows change in traditional work arrangements. Driverless cars or autonomous vehicles as they're called are coming fast. So, what'll happen to Uber and truck drivers? Great question. No one really knows. However, their work, careers, and jobs will be disrupted. Maybe, Uber drivers may evolve into automation co-pilots.

Work Lesson Earned: Key questions arise: How are large and global companies adapting to disruption? How is government adapting? Finally, how are you going to adapt. Large companies viscerally understand they don't want be the buggy whip manufacturer of the autonomous age.

KILLER APP ECONOMY

Don't just buy a new video game, make one. Don't just download the latest app, help design it. Don't just play on your phone, program it.
Barack Obama – President

"Disruption is a predictable pattern across many industries in which fledgling companies use new tech to offer cheaper and inferior alternatives to products sold by established players" said the *New York Times* a few years ago.[102] Startups don't compete based on high quality products or cheaper services. They compete with killer apps, tech platforms, and new business models.

Think Toyota taking on Detroit decades ago with higher quality vehicles. Autonomous self-driving vehicles are doing the same to self-driven vehicles. It all started with an app.

An opportunity over the past few years is creating apps and other services that match labor demand with service or product supply. These simple inventions changed entire industry sectors. In this sharing economy, Vucans and companies have underutilized services, products, and spaces. For example Airbnb sells underutilized housing space and Uber sells underutilized vehicle space as part of the sharing economy. The obvious example is Uber, the car sharing service that was founded in San Francisco 2009. The traveler just clicks an app to find an available car and negotiates the flat fee with the drive.

Work Lesson Earned: Airbnb initially called itself "a social website that connects people who have space to share with those who are looking for a place to stay." These peer-to-peer platforms have scaled because there's no middle Vucan to add friction between the buyer and seller. These platforms have 0 marginal cost for adding, distributing, and scaling services. In other words, they can add a room or add a new person to a ride at almost no overhead in terms of Vucan, power, and brick-and-mortar overhead. In other words, fewer core Vucans are required to start and scale a business using tech to balance supply and demand at ever shorter time frames. What's your idea for a killer app?

CUSTOMER'S OR EMPLOYER'S BUSINESS MODEL

Either you drive disruption or you're outpaced by it.

Porsche – Auto Company

I give lots of professional talks. I ask attendees: "how many of you know your company's business model?" Less than 10% do. Why does it matter if you know your customer's or employer's work model? It may follow the Handy model or a variant.

Vucans can tell me what they do and what department they're in. But, they don't know the company's, business unit, or department's business model. These Handy workers (middle and outer rings) are expendable if there's an economic blip.

Why is this question important? Well, your customer's or employer's business model defines your work model. It tells you where you're in the food chain, value stream, and value hierarchy. Knowing where you are, you make choices based on your risk profile. Questions to ask your include:

- Is your company going to be around next year and five years?
- Are you or your process part of your organization's inner, middle, or outer rings (Handy model).
- If your process is not part of the organizational core, then what's the chance it will be outsourced?
- If you're a middle manager, what does the organization want to do with your department or activities?
- If you're a middle ring Vucan, a project consultant, what's critical to your customer?
- What skills are critical to your customer and what's it willing to pay for them?
- What other key questions should you ask?

Work Lesson Earned: If you don't know your company's business model, you don't know how the company's makes money and you don't know how to add value to the core. If you don't know how to add value, make sure you're not ultimately expendable. Sorry, about the bad news. However, that's the way it is.

WHAT'S YOUR PROCESS?

Sometimes we make the process more complicated than we need to. We will never make a journey of a thousand miles by fretting about how long it will take or how hard it will be. We make the journey by taking each day step by step and then repeating it again and again until we reach our destination.
Joseph B. Wirthlin – Author

Process is pretty much how repetitive and core work gets done in most organizations and is the most vulnerable to automation. Organizations are usually focusing on core work and leaning-out through 'relentless' automation.

Every organization performs a sequence of activities to produce a product or offer a service. These activities add value to customers who continue purchasing the company's products and services. These value-adding activities provide income to satisfy shareholders, provide employment, and ensure the company continues to be viable.

Profitability is king (OK – queen) The goal for all commercial companies is to make a profit for investors. Process management, which include automation, project management, safety, environmental compliance, six sigma, lean, quality improvement, and other operational excellence initiatives, is critical to streamlining a business to profitability. Most if not all global companies are great at this. They also make their organizations less bureaucratic and transparent. They have standardized and controlled their operations and supply chains.

All large companies are following a similar process as the CEO of PepsiCo said:

> "Our second set of priorities ... involves becoming more capable, leaner, more agile and less bureaucratic, ... In doing so, we will drive down cost and that enables us to plow the savings back into the business to develop, scale, and sharpen core capabilities that drive even greater efficiency and effectiveness creating a virtuous cycle."[103]

Work Lesson Earned: The future challenge will involve bringing Vucans on board with all the changes. Employees will need to be calmed about change (not disruption). Women and technology will need to be integrated into organizations. Operations will have to be environmentally friendly. This will involve institutionalizing RBPS and RBDM in all functions. Companies will have to reframe work as safer and more enjoyable using smart machines as a work partner.

SELF-MANAGEMENT - YOUR NEXT STEPS

- Are you a core process worker or do you support the core (think of Handy's model)?
- What do you think of Handy's ½ x 2 x 3 rule of corporate fitness?
- What do you like and don't like about the model?
- Are you in the inner, middle or outer ring of the Handy model?
- Are there any middle ring consultants who are paid a premium in your organization? What do they do?
- What are your organization's or customer's core processes?
- What do you do at work and why is it value-adding?
- What are your core competencies – or what do you do best?
- Are you using your skills or core competencies in your work?
- Are your core competencies aligned with your organization's or customer's core processes?
- Have you gone through an organizational transformation or reengineering?
- What happened to you and how did you feel about what happened?
- Have you recently transformed or reengineered your career or skills?
- What would you do if you had to develop marketable skills in six months?
- Have you ever thought of developing a new career, working in a startup, or finding a new job?
- What would be your next steps if you wanted to explore the above options?

PROJECTS

-

GIG-WORK

Many of us think that our day-to-day work is our function or job title. In reality, we spend most of our work time doing projects. What does a project look like? A project can be software team, orchestra, or movie production team. For example, most movies are projectized by a team of Vucans consisting of writers, directors, actors, studio, distribution company, extras, accountants, and many other folks.

Roger L. Martin, a work guru, explains the importance of projects:

> "You know, every Monday morning from 8:00 am to 9 am, you'd have a meeting, that could be considered as flat and routine. But at least 80% and probably closer to 95% of your meetings are an amalgam of projects – a portfolio of projects. … The average person living in one of those buildings thinks my life is this regular job and then I have these damn projects which get in the way of my regular job."[104]

Gig-workers and side-hustlers are project workers. In America the share of temporary workers, contractors and freelancers in the workforce rose from 10.1% in 2005 to 15.8% in 2015. Gig-work, side-hustles, and even core repetitive work are mainly project-based.

Project work can be a challenge for Vucans that can't or don't self-manage. Why? It's based on getting small and large tasks done on time and budget. Individual project monitoring can be onerous if not surveillance like. Any project variances and risks are known and reported to everyone. Keeping on the project's critical path is everyone's responsibility and any deviation results in monitoring, corrective actions, and if these continue replacement. Not a fun life.

VUCAN DRIVERS – PROJECTS

Old School	New School
Full time work	Gig (alternative) work
Ad hoc project rules	Cost, schedule, quality project rules
Sequential projects	Agile projects
Core work	Project and gig-work
Large organizations	Nimble & small organizations
Project manager	Project steward and juggler
Project direction	Project administration
Authoritarian project manager	Collaborative project manager
Project failure	Project success
Functional worker	Creative worker
Life lesson learned	Work lesson earned
Ladder career metaphor	Web career metaphor
Process work	Taskified work
Proceduralized & standardized	Adaptive execution
Clear solid lines of authority	Dispersed authority & responsibility
Ad hoc inspection	Continual monitoring and assurance
Cost, schedule, and quality control	Risk variance management
Project management	Risk management
Project & team management	Self-management

PROJECTS @ RISK

Is there one right type of work structure or organization for a company? The current favorite is a projectized structure. Peter Drucker, the eminent management expert, said: 'every organization in the developed countries will have to be designed for a specific task, time, and place'. In other words, work and organizations will be projectized along lines that reflect their purpose and function of what work needs to be done.

A project can be an Uber trip. Or, a project can be sending a person to the moon or anything in between. The idea behind projectizing is to treat work as integrated tasks that have be completed on time, on budget, with high quality, and within scope, while satisfying multiple stakeholders.

See if the following makes sense? Bosses want work done cheaper, faster and better. VUCA 'work entropy' can result in the unraveling of **Working It** principles and practices. Our usual response when VUCA reaches a crisis stage is to panic. We transform processes, downsize Vucans indiscriminately, or disrupt organizational cultures. Crisis management doesn't work over the long-term.

Project work changes work assumptions. For example, traditional management hierarchies and functional silos predominate organizations but evolve in projectized organizations. Projectizing work has been growing steadily, may be exponentially, during the last several years. Why? Vucans from different parts of the organization, suppliers, and even countries must work effectively and efficiently 24-7. As well, many Vucans work virtually.

Managing by projects is hot - blistering hot! Most gig and side-hustle work are project based. Roger L. Martin, a current work guru, says:

> "My advocacy vis-a-vis projects is that the entire decision factory should be thought of as nothing but projects. Projects, projects, projects and more projects; managers should organize their life around projects." [105]

Work Lesson Earned: Is there a better way to control our work and life in an increasingly VUCA world? And, is there a simpler way to make sense and structure of work when things must get done on time? Yes, it's through risk-based, project management.

GET'ER DONE – PROJECT BEST PRACTICES

Many [business] people focus on what is static, black and white. Yet great algorithms can be rewritten. A business process can be defined better. A business model can be copied. But the speed of execution is dynamic within you and can never be copied. When you have an idea, figure out the pieces you need quickly, go to market, believe in it, and continue to iterate.
Gurbaksh Chahal – Entrepreneur

Managing by projects is not new. Earliest homo sapiens had to gather food, hunt for food, build shelter, and propagate their clans. Each activity had a beginning and end with a specific work-driven purpose. Sounds like a project to me.

Architectural, accounting, engineering, and consulting have been doing projects for years. Let's look at key project practices:

- **Specific objective.** The result, objective, or deliverable (think execution) may be reducing nonconformances by 50%, building a bridge, making 10 cold calls a day, taking the kids to the zoo, designing an ad, or planning a party. Meeting project objectives is the equivalent of performance and risk management.
- **Satisfy stakeholders.** The completion of a project is often not good enough. It must be completed on time, on budget, and satisfy many stakeholders. Satisfying stakeholders is customer management.
- **Specific start date.** The project starts at an agreed upon time. 'Do as you say and say as you do' is an example of self-management.
- **Defined date.** The project may end when the goal has been achieved or when all resources have been consumed. Or, a project may evolve into an ongoing process of continuous improvement. Finishing the project on time and on budget is an example of risk management.
- **Resources.** Resources, such as equipment and monies, are required to complete the project. Managing project resources efficiently and effectively is fundamental to project management.
- **Practices.** Vucans or teams must have the skills to complete the project successfully. Ensuring project team member have the requisite knowledge, skills, and abilities is knowledge management.

Work Lesson Earned: All critical project elements map one-to-one to **Working It** critical practices. Why? Companies want to get things done faster, better, and cheaper. This is the new normal for Vucans who can self-manage.

GIG-WORK MODELS

Basically, I live to do gigs.
Amy Winehouse - Singer

Gig-work is project work. Let's look at a few statistics about gig-work:

- 94% of American jobs created between 2005 and 2015 were for 'alternative work' (gig-work).[106]
- 36% of U.S. Vucans participate in the gig economy through their primary or secondary jobs."[107]
- Work continues to undergo seismic disruptionss with 70 million American Vucans now self-employed or doing informal work, which is a number expected to continue rising.[108]
- In the U.S., two-thirds of gig-workers are men and most would welcome fulltime, core employment. In many countries, this is often a higher number.[109]

Think of the Uber, Airbnb, and similar business models. These companies own their IP and platform. They do not own vehicles or lodging facilities. Their business model aggregates gig-workers who own unused vehicles or space. We also have subscription business models. You may pay a monthly fee for clothes, razors, shirts, and almost any consumable product and service.

Gig-work and new peer-to-peer economy does provide opportunities for new businesses.   In this new economy, hotels and lodging companies must reposition and rebrand themselves in terms of offering experiences and other attractors to tourists. A new brand of consultant has been invented that offers hotels and new revenue models to attract guests with new experiences and new value offerings

Work Lesson Earned: Customers and users want freedom of choice. Gig-work will increase to supply customers with new products and services. Got any creative ideas for gig-work?

SIDE-HUSTLE ECONOMY

We are living through a fundamental transformation in the way we work.
PwC Report

Companies don't offer lifelong employment opportunities and guarantees. Vucans must look out for #1 doing DIY work. You got a full-time gig, but need extra money for fun or the new kid. Or, you want to diversify your income with multiple project gigs. Everyone seems to have a side-hustle in this new work economy.

Over the last 10 years, there has been a huge growth in creative gig-work. Gig-workers are called independent workers, freelancers contingent workers, creative workers, project workers, or itinerant labor. The common element to many of these creatives is they involve knowledge work. Gig-workers can be coders, engineers, consultants, builders, barbers, truck drivers, lawyers, and almost any type of worker.

How does the typical gig-work? The gig-worker may have an unused asset such as a vehicle to offer personalized, on-demand services. An online platform brings customer and gig-worker together to provide a seamless online interaction. The platform takes a percentage of the negotiated deal usually 5 to 10% of the total amount of the transaction.

We're seeing the online gig platforms following a traditional disruptive model of providing a service or product with a relatively low value, but moving upstream to provide higher-value project based services and products.   Gig-work or the side-hustle is also a global phenomenon. Work needs to be done. Vucans need money. Work is contracted out. Risk-takers are starting ventures. The percentage of gig-workers varies by country. Gig-work is rising throughout the world. Most gigs are short term and project based.

Work Lesson Earned: How do you know if you're choosing the right side-hustle. Great question. There's no easy answer. What's your risk appetite, unused asset, knowledge, time, and effort. It involves your RBPS and RBDM. What do you require, want, and expect of a gig?

YOUR SIDE-HUSTLE

Always have a side-hustle.
Fortune Magazine

A side-hustle can be thought of as a decision to hedge work risks. If your main gig doesn't pay enough; you don't like your main gig; you're bored; or you may be displaced by automation, what do you do? Get a side-hustle or gig-work to hedge your risks. Your side-hustle is actualizing the Brand You to do desirable work based on your risk appetite, prosperity mantra, and work gospel.

The on-demand economy is creating disruption through wealth inequality, which leads to work and income disparities. The on-demand economy allows you to be your own boss, choose work you want to do, choose your own hours, and projects to work on based on an agreed rate.

The side-hustle happens in almost any type of work. The gig economy is happening not only with low-end services such as cleaning houses and mowing lawns, but includes by lawyers, engineers and coders.

For example, the gig economy is disrupting computer coding. Software projects in the past required legions of coders and a team of project managers. Smart entrepreneurs discovered that by chunking code into smaller pieces, they could get freelance developers throughout the world to bid on bite-sized chunks of code. This reduced costs and saved time for clients. We're seeing communities of freelance professionals and consultants offering services at a fraction of the cost of big name consultancies and law firms.

Is the side-hustle working for everyone? Too early to tell. However, one result of the side-hustle disruption may be the specialization of work. Professionals may focus on doing one task very well and will be paid accordingly.

Work Lesson Earned: Our mantra for readers: Think different. Do different. Live different. Work different. In many ways, this is the mantra of Silicon Valley startups.

UPSIDE TO GIG-WORK

I can't imagine doing an hour-long dramatic series because it's so much work. A sitcom is a wonderful gig. You work from 10 to 4 every day, it's fun, and you get to live at home.
John Lithgow – Actor

The rules of work are not fully understood as work is done throughout the world on an on-demand basis. On-demand is an emerging economic model based on short-term labor. On-demand work is more prevalent as Vucans find new ways to make a living based on personal principles and best practices.

There are a lot of benefits to gig-work. The creative can decide what type of work he or she will do. The creative has the option to decide how much she will make working for companies with shared worked beliefs. The hourly rate is usually higher than full-time employment.

In a booming economy, gig-work and side-hustles are a great alternative. Why? Gig-work allows a knowledge worker or a creative to be empowered and in control. Vucan creatives have in-demand skills. These Vucans have options. They own and control their work future. The challenge of a new project. Increased income. Risk satisfaction of new work. They develop new skills and become adaptable. Most important, they evolve into 'hybrid workers'.

Work Lesson Earned: The following story from the U.S. Navy illustrates the power of 'hybrid work':

> "The LCS was the first class of Navy ship that, because of technological change and the high cost of personnel, turned away from specialists in favor of 'hybrid sailors' who have the ability to acquire skills rapidly. It was designed to operate with a mere 40 souls on board—one-fifth the number aboard comparably sized 'legacy' ships and a far cry from the 350 aboard a World War II destroyer. The small size of the crew means that each sailor must be like the ship itself: a jack of many trades and not, as 240 years of tradition have prescribed, a master of just one."[110]

DOWNSIDE TO GIG-WORK

With every gig we have to prove ourselves better than the night before.
Ronnie Wood – Rolling Stones member of the band

Is gig-work right for you in the on-demand economy? A few critical questions arise: What's your risk appetite? Do you like people? Do you have a special skill, knowledge, IP, or talent?

Gig-work can be challenging and risky. What happens if you want to work full time instead of working intermittently, selling time and materials as an independent contractor. Gig-work can be isolating, unstable, and emotionally taxing.

Freedom and flexibility is balanced against income fluctuation and job insecurity. Gig-work does not include retirement, unemployment benefits, and health care, which add risk to the on-demand worker. Gig-work offers fewer worker protections, which may not be fully understood and have not been legislated.

And, what will gig-work look like when the economy is flat or in a recession? If you have generic skills in a down economy, then gig-work will have less demand at a lower rate. There are times when there's no work in the pipeline. There's usually little safety.

Work Lesson Earned: Gig-work such as driving for Uber is getting a lot of looks. Huge supply of cars and static demand have driven Uber wages below minimum wage in some areas. *New York Times* reported that Uber gig-work income has dropped 53% between 2013 and 2017. It's then a race to the bottom in terms of income. And as a matter of fact, this has happened in many cities that allowed Uber or Lyft to operate without any regulation. There's a lot to say about cities allowing regulated taxis and unionized drivers.

PROJECT WORK

In a projectized organization, such as a startup, work is organized into project teams that form and disband when work is finished. Each Vucan evolves into a project professional responsible for getting work done on time, on budget while satisfying stakeholders. Think of this as the essence of self-management. Often, there are no permanent job titles or permanent job assignments. There are few bosses and job titles. Vucan teams and individuals self-manage their work.

We've been discussing self-management in **Working It** because most work will projectized. Why?

- Customers want faster, cheaper, and better.
- Work is core-processed and projectized.
- Product life cycles are halved and are shrinking further.
- Vucan managers must do more with less.
- Cross-functional, virtual project teams do more work.
- Project manager replaces middle manager.
- Work is chunked into projects and sub-projects.

The project work environment is not for everyone. Responsibility for work may not come with authority. Project atmosphere is intense with tight deadlines. Flat project hierarchy places a premium on Vucans with ideas who can execute quickly. Status and salary are earned and based on real value-added contributions.

Work Lesson Earned: Projects are your Vucan learning laboratory. Projects offer special benefits. Special projects are critical for your professional development. They offer you the opportunity to learn new things. They offer you access to higher management where you can reveal your value proposition or help you develop a higher value proposition. It's a great learning platform for yourself and for future work.

There are few really good books on project work. But, join the Project Management Institute (PMI) to learn project work tools. Get certified as a Project Management Professional® (PMP) or as a Certified Enterprise Risk Manager® (CERM).

PROJECTIZED WORKPLACE OF THE FUTURE

Do not try to do everything. Do one thing well.
Steve Jobs – Apple Founder

The videogame business is an example of an industry adopting project-based work and points to the *Future of Work*. Casey O'Donnell, a game developer and game-studies professor at Michigan State University, says videogame industry "is a decade ahead of where a lot of other industries are going." [111]

Psyonix is a projectized organization and is typical of the *Future of Work*. Psyonix dreams up new games and even car designs. Each product requires software development and project management. The company uses a network of project contractors (middle ring) throughout the world to develop software, translate its games into foreign languages, conduct quality control, handle customer service, and transfer the software to new platforms. Psyonix in the meanwhile has amassed 25 million players in less than two years using the project work model.

The CEO of Psyonix says: "the smaller we can be the better." Think lean. Think fast. Be agile. And most importantly, be profitable. Psyonix contractors are called its liquid workforce (middle ring). Why? They can be turned on and off like a faucet. And both parties can benefit from this arrangement. Psyonix can scale as required by hiring layers of project managers, contractors, and subcontractors. And, contractors can make a lot of money and have the freedom working on a temporary basis or on a project-by-project basis. [112]

Companies say the result is just-in-time work fueled with human capital. By outsourcing low-value work or renting high-value expertise needed for a short time, game makers like Psyonix can focus on what they do best. Smaller companies such as high tech startups are following this work model. For example, the company that designed the hit video game Rocket League which pits jet powered, race cars against one another in an online soccer match only has 81 employees.

Work Lesson Earned: "As outsourcing sweeps through almost every industry in the U.S., the videogame business looks a lot like the workplace of the future. A lean core of in-house employees focuses on the most important jobs, with the rest hired out to layers of contractors and subcontractors. Outside workers come and go based on project cycles." [113]

CHUNKING WORK

Chunking makes our brains more efficient. The more you can chunk something, the faster and easier you can process it. Wayne Gretzky had chunked hockey like no one before or since. Talented people have supremely chunked whatever they become talented at doing.
Keven Maney – Columnist & Designer

Project work is popular because it can be taskified, specifically chunked, managed, and controlled into small units. Why? Project management is great for mitigating schedule (time) risk, cost (money) risk, and quality (satisfied customers) risk.

Vucan projects and programs are chopped up into mini projects and even tasks. This happened in software development, engineering, construction, automotive design, and manufacturing. For example, an automobile can be chunked into assembly, sub-assembly, component, and part projects. Then, software can be integrated into each level of the automobile. Each level of the automotive hierarchy can be project managed.

This is the basis of lean startups. Agile project management is based on the idea that work in a startup can be broken down into smaller chunks and even these chunks can be broken down into sub chunks. Each chunk is project managed so that the larger project can be finished on time, on budget, and within scope.

Much in the same way, complex process work (inner ring) can be broken down into components. For example, software development may have architects, designers, coders, QC testers, and project managers.

What does this projectized future hold for Vucans? Workers completing the work order are self-managing professionals and among the best in their fields. They do the work economically, effectively, and efficiently. Their output in performance may even be better than the specialized worker. And in a global and virtual work world, they can do this work almost anywhere in the world.

Work Lesson Earned: Here's the work challenge. Bite-sized work can be parceled out to low-paid workers throughout the world. They can bid for the work, but can be a race to the bottom since work goes to the low bidder. Who will be the winners and losers is the VUCA economy? Many of the winners will be tech savvy Vucans who want to learn new topics just-in-time. The losers may be lower-level workers who require a minimum wage just to sustain themselves.

PROJECT MANAGER OR JUGGLER

You can't move fast and break things if the things you might break are people.
Clara Vu - Engineer

In this new work environment, what's the title and role of the Vucan who brings all the resources together in the project team? Is the Vucan a project manager, leader, coach, or facilitator? Or, maybe all of these based on context and situation.

Project work leadership is abstract, touchy-feely, and frankly difficult. The projectized organization looks and feels a lot different than the managerial, hierarchal work model. In the hierarchal model, work got done through one Vucan telling another what to do and how to do it. Even the term 'project manager' evokes images of one Vucan dictating to thousands of ready minions the direction of a grandiose project, such as moving mountains, building airports, or dredging rivers. Manager implies a hierarchal relationship where the boss is responsible for planning, organizing, staffing, and controlling all project activities. Decisions are based on power and position.

In the projectized model, work gets done differently. A project is organized around a lead Vucan, who may be called project leader instead of manager. The project leader facilitates and administrates more than actively manages the project. While a project may have started with one Vucan who had the vision and authority to push onwards, one-person management has been replaced by team driven, project leadership. The project leader may not have sufficient resources or even authority to tell someone to do something. The leader must rely on influence, web of preexisting relationships, and goodwill established through prior work.

What's in it for the Vucan in the projectized work relationship? Each project allows you to gain additional experience and exposure to a company's operations, processes, and products. You're a team leader or sometimes a virtual team participant. You're adding value to the organization, team, and finally to your career portfolio.

Work Lesson Earned: PM work is squishy – lots of opportunity, little authority, and lots of responsibility. There are few step-by-step manuals that show the path to project success. PM's are CEO's of a work center. It's great experience and exposure to Vucans to develop and practice their skills.

ORCHESTRA PROCESS & PROJECT WORK MODEL

Understand the culture of the new company (with which you are joining or negotiating) and its standards of what is reasonable.

James Nunan - Business person

What's the best metaphor for defining the project structure and process for getting lean and agile work done? It may be an orchestra.

An orchestra does both process and project work. Let's first look at the orchestra's process work. An orchestra is a metaphor for process excellence. The orchestra is usually known for a critical body of musical work that it plays spectacularly and repetitively. This is the orchestra's value-added process differentiator. The musical body of work is the orchestra's unique selling proposition. For example, opera lovers will go to Milan for it's great orchestra, opera singers, operatic acoustic venue, and Verdi's body of work.

The orchestra is composed of different musical sections like woodwinds, brass, strings, and percussion. These musical sections can be compared to processes with different instruments like machines. This is very similar to any office or factory with its functional process teams and suppliers of key products. The goal of each musical section, whether it's woodwinds, strings, or brass is to consistently blend with other musical sections. Each professional may add his or her interpretation to the music.

The orchestra is also a project. Each time the orchestra gets a new gig it works together on a specific composer's music. Think of this as a special project. The orchestra is composed of project team members, each of whom is gifted, has a unique talent, and has a distinct way of delivering music to satisfied customers. Usually, each player is a superstar in his or her right. Each musician adds value and pleasure to the theater goer. Each orchestra musician is chosen because of unique abilities and talents. The musician must pass an audition based on talent and ability. Once chosen, the musician must rehearse and continue to build upon his or her abilities.

Work Lesson Earned: Hollywood movies or orchestras are a hybrid process and project work model. They consist of core process workers and project workers. Which work model works best for you?

PROJECT CONDUCTOR <=> RISK MANAGER

True genius resides in the capacity for evaluation of uncertain, hazardous, and conflicting information.
Winston Churchill – English Prime Minister

Project management is risk management. If projects were simple, straightforward, and had no risk of cost, schedule, scope, and quality variances, then a project manager wouldn't be necessary. I like the model of orchestra conductor as project manager and risk manager.

Henry Mintzberg, the famous writer and academic, captured the essence of project risk:

> "The great myth is the manager as orchestra conductor. It's this idea of standing on a pedestal and you wave your baton and accounting comes in, and you wave it somewhere else and marketing chimes in with accounting, and they all sound very glorious. But management is more like orchestra conducting during rehearsals, when everything is going wrong."[114]

The orchestra conductor is a project team leader and risk coach rather than an authoritarian manager. The conductor leads a group of professionals who are proficient with their instruments and know their individual capabilities. The modern conductor interprets the musical score and shapes the orchestra's sound so it pleases the audience. The conductor then leads by interpretation, example, and strength of personality rather than by barking orders.

What about the ass-hole or control freak project manager of a death march project? This Vucan is a Theory X authoritarian 'my way or the highway boss'. They're very good in getting project getting done on budget and on schedule unfortunately with strewn bodies.

Work Lesson Earned: A project manager has a tough job. If a PM can't bring in projects on time and within budget, then this person is replaced. It is a game of project musical chairs. Few do it well. The PM is reacting to changing stakeholder requirements, demanding schedules, cost pressures, and signing off on project objectives the PM knows can't be achieved. There is little time to think about the project. The PM is simply reacting to daily events, not responding thoughtfully. So if you develop strong project management and risk management skills, this is something you can use throughout your life.

STARTUPS AS PROJECT WORK

You like to do project work. But, do you have the right risk profile? What's your risk appetite? Are you risk-taking, risk-sensitive, or risk-averse? If you like to take risks, one option is to strike out on your own and start a business or work on a startup. Startup work is all about extreme self-management. If you have a good track record, you'll attract investment like flowers attract bees.

What do I mean? I'm a risk taker. I'm a rush junkie. If I've got a great commercial idea, I want to monetize it. What about you?

What percentage of American households includes someone who has started, tried to start, or helped fund a small business? One percent, five, or even ten percent? Well guess again! Thirty-seven percent of American households are involved with entrepreneurship, startups, small business, gig-work, or side-hustles. Entrepreneurs were once considered Vucans who couldn't work in a big company because they were seen as business misfits, even a little disreputable.

Let's look at startups. Startup work is not for the weak of heart. Up to half of small businesses don't make it past two years. Joseph Schumpeter, the economist called the process 'creative destruction.' Ideas for new products and services develop, companies form, they grow, products are altered or new products are developed, and the company morphs again.

As a startup founder and workaholic, startups can be brutal. Gary Pisano, a Harvard Business School Professor, captured the startup angst:

> "But, there's a harsh reality of innovative cultures. They are not much fun. There's little tolerance for incompetence, they are extremely disciplined, they involve high degrees of personal accountability, and they are brutally candid places. Not everyone will thrive we would add one further thing: most folks don't thrive."[115]

Work Lesson Earned: Only self-managing Vucans can survive a startup. I've started a number of startups. Some tanked, others broke even, and one or two actually made money. This is after years of very long - many 80-hour weeks and little pay. Would I do it again? You bet, in a heartbeat - no in a nanosecond! Why? It's in my DNA. I'm a risk taker. I love the freedom to fail or succeed. I love the rush of doing my own thing.

DIY WORK

Your work should be an extended hobby.
Richard Saul Wurman - Writer and Thinker

Entrepreneurship, 'doing it your way', is in. The startup dream is alive and well as attested by many who want to immigrate to the U.S. A new meritocracy is found inside and outside companies. You're rewarded for your ideas, initiative, perseverance, performance, and results. Failure is tolerated as long as it's part of the **Work Lesson Earned**. Organizational disruptors are seen as future leaders. Small business entrepreneurs are seen as job-creators, adders of value, creators, and business icons.

What's the #1 tip for making it big in project, gig, or startup work? I like Wurman's above quote. If you like project work and it's what drives you, you'll do great.

The second huge question is: what should you do if you can't monetize an extended hobby? The internet has created many new opportunities where a person can leverage a business model and scale quickly. Millennial Vucans are more inclined to take risks and challenge existing work and business paradigms.

What's great about disruption is that lots of new and nichey opportunities are created. Your Plan B may be to: Fill a need. Scratch an itch. Reduce the pain. Answer a tough question. Eliminate critical risks. Do simple what's hard. Make something cheaper, faster, of better.

Schumacher about 30 years ago wrote a simple and paradigm-busting book called **Small is Beautiful**. This was a breakthrough book when the business world was thinking big is better. Today, small means entrepreneurial, startup, paradigm busting, vibrant, lean, agile, customer-driven, free, sustainable and profitable. Big, slow, hindering, plodding, and corporate are dead.

Vucan work rules have also changed. Vucans can work at home or Starbuckies. Vucans are blending work and family. They have a side-hustle that can become full time work.

Work Lesson Earned: I'm a huge believer on making my way as a small business owner and being the master of my destiny. Family-engaged, DIY, and small are the new work model for those who want to control their work futures, do good, have a balanced work-life. Look at the many big companies who are struggling mightily to shed their legacy systems, processes, and culture to be like a startup.

AGILE PROJECTS

Software projects fail for one of two general reasons: the project team lacks the knowledge to conduct a software project successfully or the project team lacks the resolve to conduct a project effectively.

Steve McConnell – Software Engineer & Writer

The *New York Times* a few years ago had an article called 'The New Workplace Is Agile and Nonstop'. Agile project management is an iterative and incremental approach to project work based on flexibility and collaboration.

Large companies want to be agile, innovative, and fast. The challenge is many large companies have a legacy culture and internal systems that promote the status quo rather than agility. Not good for innovation, particularly software development

Large and small companies in government and the private sector like agile projects. Projects have a hard beginning and a hard end. Progress can be measured. Resources are allocated. Vucans know what to do and when to do it. And if there are differences in scope, quality, cost, or schedule, these can be corrected relatively quickly.

Speed is a key attribute of agile projects. Project teams may be virtual with members throughout the world. Communications are instantaneous. Workers have flexible hours.

Vucans were generally hired, trained, remunerated, and promoted for knowing and doing the things in their original job description. This is a challenge in projectized work environments, where work is discontinuous and generalized. Workers need new knowledge, skills and abilities. Core workers are expected to have general expertise and core specialization knowledge.

Work Lesson Earned: The kicker in agile projects is Vucans are expected to be 'hybrid workers' available 24 x 7.

PROJECT WORK TIPS AND TOOLS

It takes no talent to work hard.
Tim S. Grover – Author

I've been a project consultant for 30 years and have written best-selling books. Here are my top tips and tools:

Work Lessons Earned:

- **Know your value proposition.** What separates you from the rest of the Vucans? Then price your services accordingly. I differentiate consultants into 4 categories: 1. How; 2. What; 3. Why; and 4. Who consultants. How consultants ($200/hr.) know how to do something right. What consultants ($300/hr.) know what to do right? Why consultants ($400/hr.) know why the right work must be done right. Who consultants ($500-$1000/hr.) know who pays for doing the right work right.

- **Add real and perceived value.** Commodity consulting goes for about $200/hour. Move up the how, what, why, and who consulting curve to offer higher real and perceived customer value. How consultants are skilled technicians. What consultants are skilled managers? Why consultants are skilled communicators. Who consultants are skilled leaders and politicians. Who consultants offer clients peace of mind in today's VUCA world.

- **Differentiate yourself.** How do you differentiate yourself from the rest of the project consulting and work Vucans? The differentiator is what makes you different. This is your 'value proposition.'

- **Reinvent yourself.** I used to reinvent myself every 7 years – my half-life. That's too long. I do it every two to three years. It's critical to stay ahead of the VUCA curve.

- **Update your Brand You.** Personal brand management (Brand You) is what consulting is all about these days. Look out for your #1. Your employer won't. You need to update continuously your brand, skills, contacts, knowledge, etc.

- **Develop a killer new process or product and write a book about it.** Another thing I've learned about consulting is that there's a linear correlation between visibility > credibility > marketability > brandability > billability. It's pretty simple. Visibility through a thought leadership blogs, vlogs, social media, books, or clever methodology leads to your marketability, employability, and billability. It's that simple.

LEARN FROM YOUR PROJECTS

A bad habit never disappears miraculously; it's an undo-it-yourself project.
Abigail Van Buren – Self Help Guru

I've project managed $200M projects. I've had some jobs come in on budget, in scope, and on schedule. I've had projects fail miserably and been fired. I've had to kill projects. I think I've made almost every project mistake. There are things I've learned on why projects fail:

- Bad politics.
- Wrong project manager or team members on the wrong project.
- Prima donna or maverick team members.
- 'Hole in the wall' offices, few resources, and bad facilities.
- 'Death march' project mentality.
- Reinvent the universe project objectives.
- 'Throw more people' at the project attitude.
- 'We're all behind you' attitude by executive management and stakeholders.
- Gold plating requirements.
- Project creep.
- Wish lists and product goodies (scope creep).
- 'I wanted it' yesterday attitude.
- Fuzzy understandings - fuzzy everything.
- 'It's their job' attitude.
- 'Plan is a 4-letter word' attitude.
- 'Silver-bullet' attitude.
- Too many surprises and gotcha's.
- Few risk-controls.
- 'I know it all' attitude.

I've been on both sides of the above mistakes – perpetrator and victim. Quick takeaway: it's better to be the perpetrator and be right. You get to fight another day. However, if you find yourself on the perpetrator making mistakes or the victim side of the equation, start thinking of your Plan B's.

Work Lesson Earned: Read good books: **Career Survival**, Machiavelli's **The Prince**, and Lao Tzu's **Art of War**. You'll get a different perspective on the project game and learn how to play another day.

PROJECT WORK FUTURES

It takes half your life before you discover life is a do-it-yourself project.
Napoleon Hill – Self-Help Author

In a projectized organization, work is organized into project teams that form and disband when work is finished. Each Vucan evolves into a project professional responsible for getting work done on time and on budget while satisfying stake-holders. Often, there are no permanent job titles or permanent job assignments. There are few bosses and job titles. Teams and individuals self-manage their work.

This work environment (middle ring) is not for everyone. The atmosphere is intense with tight deadlines. The flat hierarchy places a premium on Vucans with ideas who can execute and monetize. Status is earned and salary is based on real value-added contributions.

A project is defined, authorized, and resourced. Project is broken down to specific tasks each of which are linked. Work is broken down into specific tasks or fragments around a project. Sometimes, this is taskifying or crowd sourcing work. Think of this as creative or knowledge piece work. This is the basic project work model

Work Lesson Earned: Vucans are moving to project management because:

- High risk, high return.
- Rapid upward mobility.
- CEO of your team.
- Customers want faster, cheaper, and better.
- Product life cycles are halved and shrinking further.
- People must do faster, with less.
- Work is core-processed or projectized.
- Cross-functional virtual project teams do more work.
- Project manager replaces middle manager.
- Work is global and is chunked into projects and sub-projects.

SELF-MANAGEMENT - YOUR NEXT STEPS

There are two primary choices in life: to accept conditions as they exist, or accept the responsibility for changing them.
Denis Waitley - Writer

- Do you work in a projectized organization?
- Are you a project manager, lead, specialist, or support person?
- Do you want to change your project role (s)?
- If so, what are your plans to change your role (s)?
- If your project succeeds, what are your personal implications?
- If your project fails, what are your personal implications?
- Do you have the appropriate knowledge, skills, and abilities to work on key projects?
- What are your key project differentiators?
- How do you manage quality, scope, technology, schedule, and cost in your projects?
- What are your biggest project assets?
- What are your biggest project challenges?
- Do you project manage your work-life?
- Do you volunteer or are selected for highly visible new projects?
- Why or why not are you selected?
- Do you believe that project managers will replace middle managers?
- What types of project tools do you use?
- Have you done a career gap analysis?
- What are your next steps?
- Have you ever thought of starting a small business and being your own boss?
- What is your personal risk appetite in a project?
- How do you manage your project and yourself?
- What keeps you up at night regarding your projects?
- What is your personal direction and passion about projects?

FUTURE OF WORK

-

YES, THERE'S HOPE!

Shaping the *Future of Work* is up to each of us:

> "As technological breakthroughs rapidly shift the frontier between the work tasks performed by humans and those performed by machines and algorithms, global labor markets are undergoing major transformations. These transformations, if managed wisely, could lead to a new age of good work, good jobs and improved quality of life for all, but if managed poorly, pose the risk of widening skills gaps, greater inequality and broader polarization."[116]

VUCA is real because of rising expectations and limited opportunities. Unhappy Vucans are now called the precariat: "a social class .. which is a condition of existence without predictability or security, affecting (their) material or psychological welfare."[117]

It's so important that it's a political issue in many countries. Bernie Sanders, U.S. Senator running for president, distilled the *Future of Work* challenge:

> "A nation will not survive morally or economically when so few have so much and so many have so little."

While the quote applies to U.S. companies and billionaires, this truth relates to oligarchs and companies paying no taxes. We're seeing Vucan dissatisfaction and rioting in many countries

What's the answer? Understanding and getting it. Adaptability. Finally, lifelong learning. The *Future of Work* is continually learning how to work and upgrade your marketable practices. "Lifelong learning has become a mantra in American corporations as employees face pressure to stay relevant in a rapidly evolving workplace" according to the *Wall Street Journal*.[118] The challenge is figuring out what knowledge, skills, and abilities will be valuable and marketable next year and in five years. This requires a mixture of reading tea leaves and looking around corners.

VUCAN DRIVERS - FUTURE OF WORK

Old School	New School
U.S. & western work rules	Asian & Chinese work rules
Manual dexterity, endurance, and precision	Analytical thinking & innovation
Memory, verbal, auditory, & spatial abilities	Active learning & learning strategies
Management of material resources	Creativity, originality and initiative
Tech installation & maintenance	Tech design & programming
Reading, writing, math, & active listening	Critical thinking & analysis
Ladder career metaphor	Lattice career metaphor
Security	Precarity
Coordination & time management	Emotional intelligence
Visual, auditory, & speech abilities	Reasoning, problem-solving & ideation
Tech use, monitoring, & control	Systems analysis & evaluation[119]
Work continuity	Work insecurity
Long-term career	Episodic career & jobs
College degree	Nano degree or no degree required
Quality of the answers	Quality of the questions
Work for everyone	High paid work as Hunger Games
Local work	Globalized work

FUTURE OF WORK @ RISK

It isn't the changes that do you in, it's the transitions. Change is not the same as transition. Change is situational: the new site, the new boss, the new team roles, the new policy. Transition is the psychological process people go through to come to terms with the new situation. Change is external, transition is internal.

William Bridges – Work Transitions Writer

Job growth throughout the world is already uneven or even spiky. However, certain patterns are beginning to emerge. Lots of work will involve tech. Process work in the middle ring of the Handy model will evolve, decline, or disappear due to automation. Project work in the middle circle will offer competitive wages, move offshore, or disappear. Many new jobs coming at the outside circle will be low-wage at the bottom of the economic pyramid.

Handy Work Model is real and offers significant upside and down side risks:

> "... corporations across America have flocked to a new management theory: Focus on core competence and outsource the rest. The approach has made companies nimbler and more productive, and delivered huge profits for shareholders. It has also fueled inequality and helps explain why many working-class Americans are struggling even in an ostensibly healthy economy."[120]

While disruption rules, reality can suck. Vucans are challenged. The struggle is real. Vucans are not keeping up. It's estimated that about 2 billion of today's youth will be left behind due to emerging tech. These Vucans want to improve their lives. But, they don't have the basic skills and opportunities. And, many live at the wrong place at the wrong time.[121]

Work Lesson Earned: American Psychological Association regularly conducts surveys of the workforce to check satisfaction of the work environment. Not good! Big reason is companies don't want to pay for retraining. Why? Vucans can take the company's' investment in training and go elsewhere. This results in two outcomes: 1. Workers don't have the skills (Practices) necessary to succeed and 2. Workers are not mentally ready for tech disruption (Principles).

THE STRUGGLE IS REAL!

"Exhausted." "Lost". "Anxious." "Everything's a struggle." These quotes from a *Harvard Business Review* article are from Millennials (22-37 years old) who are struggling at the school-to-work transition or at work.[122] *NY Times* said:

> "In the past, workers with average skills, doing an average job, could earn an average lifestyle. But, today, average is officially over. Being average just won't earn you what it used to. It can't when so many more employers have so much more access to so much more above average cheap foreign labor, cheap robotics, cheap software, cheap automation and cheap genius. Therefore, everyone needs to find their extra — their unique value contribution that makes them stand out in whatever is their field of employment.[123]

In **Working It**, we call Millennials the 'lost work generation'? Why? The following from a *Wall Street Journal* survey captures U.S. and global work challenges:

> "American Millennials are approaching middle age in worse financial shape than every living generation ahead of them, lagging behind baby boomers and Generation X despite a decade of economic growth and falling unemployment. Hobbled by the financial crisis and recession that struck as they began their working life, Americans born between 1981 and 1996 have failed to match every other generation of young adults born since the Great Depression. They have less wealth, less property, lower marriage rates and fewer children, according to new data that compare generations at similar ages. Even with record levels of education, the troubles of Millennials have delayed traditional adult milestones in ways expected to alter the nation's demographic and economic contours through the end of the century. Millennials helped drive the number of U.S. births to their lowest levels in 32 years."[124]

Work Lesson Earned: Millennials Vucans world over have been treated specially. They have been given things. They have been fawned over. Many don't know how to fail and be resilient in a competitive VUCA world. They've had a hard time adjusting to the *Future of Work* as the Millennial quote indicates

> "When you're young coming out of college, you don't realize what you're walking into. You either perform or you don't, and you could lose your job any day. Students think it's easy-going just like school, but it's nothing like that. It's a lot more responsibility."[125]

RISE OF THE NEO LUDDITES

We have displacement and a failure to create shared prosperity, but we are not heading to an economy without human labor anytime soon.
Daron Acemoglu - MIT professor

We're on a social and *Future of Work* voyage driven by tech. And, it'll be a bumpy ride. And a lot of Vucans won't like it and don't want it.

A new tech resistance is forming. Neo Luddites are challenging the deployment of robotic, AI, and frankly all tech. The original Luddites were English textile workers in the early 19th Century that objected to the introduction of the mechanical automation of textile weaving, power looms, and spinning frames. The Luddites destroyed the mechanical looms that threatened their livelihoods. Today, neo-Luddites have the same fear of artificial intelligence, robotics, and automation eliminating their jobs.

A quick story may illustrate this: Arizona in the U.S. is the worldwide mecca for testing robotic (autonomous) vehicles. Neo Luddites have attacked driverless vehicles two dozen times with knives, rocks, and waving guns to driverless vehicles over the last two years in Arizona.

> "In ways large and small, the city (Phoenix) has had an early look at the public misgiving over the rise of artificial intelligence, with city officials hearing complaints about everything from safety to possible job losses."[126]

> "Some analysts say they expect more such behavior as the nation moves into a broader discussion about the potential for driverless cars to unleash colossal changes in American society. The debate touches on fears ranging from eliminating jobs for drivers to ceding control over mobility to autonomous vehicles."[127]

Soothsayers say new tech will change the fundamental ways you work and live much like the Industrial Revolution disrupted work early in the 19th century. Tech soothsayers predict a new industrial order based on AI in which Vucans are not prepared.

Work Lesson Earned: The history of tech follows reaction patterns such as resistance to the adoption of new ideas. Neo Luddites are the metaphor of the resistance to tech disruption and innovation because of perceived mass elimination and displacement of workers.

VUCAN LEADERSHIP

This period is like the Industrial Revolution, it's like Dickens's London, for the amount of convulsion and change, and we only recently have begun to think about it that way,
Mark Muro - Fellow at the Brookings Institution

What will managing and leading the *Future of Work* look like? No one really knows.

The true challenge will be developing new organizational structures, mindsets, and new rules of work. The logical response to VUCA is to mitigate and control risks by developing controls, establishing narrow boundary conditions, specifying specific work tools, and limiting expectations.

Why focus on risk-controls? This is the traditional and logical reaction to limiting risk exposures, consequences, and likelihood. People, process, and technology controls are designed and deployed according to the organization's risk appetite. The down-side to this approach is that Vucan's inventiveness, flexibility, and engagement can be severely thwarted.

The following excerpts from the *Future of Work Study* project describe the challenge and another possible response:

Challenge:

> "Too many leaders are willing to be out of sync with the needs of the workforce because embracing the *Future of Work*, including changing how companies are run, means higher risks, uncertainty and (perceived) loss of control of outcomes."[128]

Response:

> "Many of today's most successful ventures ... are either based on new ways of organizing and empowering people or are creating the tools for all people to empower themselves. Every company needs to stop restraining its people by holding back and risk-managing and tip-toeing around the approaches that will deliver the *Future of Work*."[129]

Work Lesson Earned: Take many of these stories to heart as you understand and decide your *Future of Work*.

RISE IN BULLSH*T WORK

Don't limit yourself. Many people limit themselves to what they think they can do. You can go as far as your mind lets you. What you believe, remember, you can achieve.
Mary Kay Ash - Entrepreneur

Almost 40% of workers according to surveys say their work and jobs make little difference to the organization, customer or marketplace. OK! So why do these jobs exist? Great question.

The Peter Principle in the 1950's stated that people in a traditional hierarchal organization rise to their 'level of incompetence' doing wasteful work. David Graeber in **Bull Sh*t Jobs** analyzes wasteful work:

> "a bullsh*t job is one that even the person doing it secretly believes need not or should not exist. That if the job, or even the whole industry, were to vanish, either it would make no difference to anyone, or the world might even be a slightly better place."[130]

Is there a list of bull sh*t jobs? No. However, we could come up with a possible list: public relations, compliance workers, supervisors, and work titles such as data wrangler for data analyst, corporate evangelist, or digital overlord for website designer.

A theme woven through this book is there are not enough high paying and satisfying jobs for Vucans worldwide. Hutchins's principle states: 'bullsh*t jobs are created to appease high worker expectations and to ensure the appearance of value-added, sustainable work'. Another way to think about bullshit jobs is in terms of what you do each day? How do you make something or create value? Are you a taker or a maker at work? Anyway you get the idea.

Work lesson Earned: Graeber asks why a job or work is done in the first place in the big picture of things? So ask yourself: Why did you write that report today? Why did the boss want that memo? So, what's the meaning and value of your work?'

BIG DATA – TODAY'S OIL

If it wasn't hard, everyone would do it. It's the hard that makes it great.
Tom Hanks – Actor

Internet of Things, known as Internet of Everything, will have toasters and re-frigerators communicating and sharing data. Multiply this by a billion results in lots of data being shared every second.

Let's look at the numbers. Seven billion Vucans inhabit this planet. Within 10 years, each Vucan will have a cell phone and personal sensors sharing information with a hospital, business, home, or supplier. Each products will have an address and share information with other machines. For example, Vucans will control homes electronically when the family is thousands of miles away. Anyway, you get the idea of big data.

The data revolution allows businesses to establish new work models that can mediate and disrupt entire sectors. Big data will also be a force of disruption and Vuca control as countries and cities surveil and control. Think Big Brother management systems generating and sharing personal data 24x7 globally.

But, what happens to the *Future of Work* with information privacy or data overload? New businesses, opportunities, and jobs will be created such as data mining and data engineering. Vucans can sift through large amounts of information, and discover trends that can be monetized. Now the downside: How are you planning to manage, interpret, and secure your personal information so it's safe?

Work Lesson Earned: You can see why big data is called today's oil or electricity. Data science is called the sexiest work of the 21st century. Data science is all about RBPS and RBDM based on large amounts data. If I were going to school today, I'd become a data scientist instead of an oil and gas engineer, which was the go-to career years ago.

AI – FRIEND OR FOE?

The development of full artificial intelligence could spell the end of the human race.
Stephen Hawking – Physicist

Alexa, my Samsung TV, and most of our connected home products can talk to me and each other. But, machine smartness is causing problems. Big Brother, smart machine (s) seem to be always recording, listening and monitoring. CCTV are always filming and surveilling. Facial recognitions systems are always scanning and identifying Vucans. These seem like a minor inconvenience, but will get more intrusive as these machines get smarter.

Ian McEwan, the English writer, recently warned:

> "We are on the verge of turning off Alexa. She [the voice-controlled smart speaker] keeps butting in on our conversations and I am rather suspicious of this listening device in the room. We might just pull the plug on her."[131]

The rules of engagement and even questions around work with machines have not been defined. And then, there's the relationship thing between Vucan and machine. Are the rules: Vucan and machine, Vucan or machine, Vucan + machine, Vucan – machine, or something not yet envisioned? The *New York Times* posed three questions about AI's impact on the *Future of Work*:

- What can it do?
- Where is it headed?
- How fast will it spread?[132]

Work Lesson Earned: Where will this go? No one knows! There's not even a relationship taxonomy to describe the work relationship with machines. Taken to a logical next step, McEway in **Machines Like Me**, describes a relationship triangle thought impossible just a few years ago: "A couple—Charlie and Miranda—find themselves in a fraught ménage-à-trois with their android, Adam."[133] He continues:

> "One of the most ethically contentious subjects of the day: the rise of artificial intelligence (AI) and a potentially uneasy co-existence of real and synthetic humans."[134]

RISK ASSURANCE

'Sunspring,' the first known screenplay written by an AI, was produced recently. It is awesome. Awesomely awful. But it's worth watching all ten minutes of it to get a taste of the gap between a great screenplay and something an AI can currently produce.
Brad Field – Screen Writer

Let's run a thought experiment? Can you imagine a pilotless commercial aircraft carrying 200 people? Pilotless airplanes have been a possibility for 20 years. However, think of the following and how you would react:

- Can you imagine looking at the pilot cabin of an aircraft looking left and right and there's no one in the cabin?
- Can you imagine visiting a machine physician for a life threatening diagnosis and no people interaction?
- Can you imagine an 80,000 pound truck traveling at 70 miles per hour on the road without a driver?
- How would you react if a robotic cop stopped you for speeding?

Does the above sound far-fetched? In a recent study, it was discovered the average pilot is flying the aircraft an average of 7 minutes. What occurs during the rest of the flight? Autopilot and other automated flight services are in control. What will happen to the pilot and co-pilot in future aircraft when automated aircraft are accepted much like automated vehicles? The role of pilots and physicians may evolve into an assurance and oversight function ensuring proper operation. The pilot monitors the automatic flight. The physician provides the human second opinion after the machine's diagnosis.

Work Lesson Learned: Assurance workers may be paid a premium for their wisdom, judgment, and humanity including their knowledge of the discipline and AI. Uber drivers could charge premium fares based on their safety record, time of day service, and special events.

EPISODIC CAREERS

You have a choice: pursue your dreams or be hired by someone else to help them fulfill their dreams.

Jay Samit – Entrepreneur

Future of Work careers may be episodic. What does episodic mean? TV programs are episodic. A TV series has individual programs or episodes, each of which is a story with beginning, middle, and end. The episodes fill in the narrative arc of the overall show.

This is similar to an episodic career where you move from opportunity-to-opportunity, project-to-project, and work-to-work until you find your true north. She offers three factors for a successful episodic career: 1. Self-knowledge; 2. Understanding the job market; and 3. Emotional resilience. In other words, you need be smart and roll with the punches.

Farai Chedeya in **Episodic Career: How to Thrive at Work in the Age of Disruption** believes:

> "Given today's pervasive anxiety, people have to make analytical decisions not just based on their paycheck and social status, but integrating their life and work and all the things that make them happy."[135]

Work Lesson Earned: The author predicts two models for work. The hopscotch career where a Vucan has a series of work episodes with a consistent theme or work that is unrelated and inconsistent. The second model of work is the slash career where Vucans have simultaneous micro-careers or different side-hustles.[136]

More work models will emerge. Write to us if you know of any at: GregH@europa.com

MANAGING AND ENGINEERING THE FUTURE OF WORK

If colleges were businesses they would be right for hostile takeovers, complete with serious cost-cutting and painful reorganizations.
US News and World Report

Overarching theme in this book is the need for lifelong, continuing education. But, few colleges are meeting this need. They seem to be frozen due to the oncoming Edupocalypse or educational disruption. They can't adapt quickly.

Just one example of change: My daughter is taking online college classes for her mechanical and robotics engineering degree. No brick and mortar - just online. Welcome to the future of education.

Let's look at two universities that hope to shape the management and technology of the *Future of Work.* Harvard Business School wants to set the benchmark on *Managing the Future of Work™.* Why?

> "The nature of work is changing. As companies grapple with forces—such as rapid technological change, shifting global product and labor markets, evolving regulatory regimes, outsourcing, and the fast emergence of the gig economy—they must overcome challenges and tap opportunities to attract, retain, and improve the productivity of their human assets. ... Tackling the changing nature of work will require companies to move beyond outdated workforce development models and human resource practices."[137]

MIT wants to develop the tech benchmark for *Engineering the Future of Work:*

> "The remarkable progression of innovations that imbue machines with human and superhuman capabilities is generating significant uncertainty and deep anxiety about the *Future of Work.* ... But there's no question that we face an urgent sense of collective concern about how to harness these technological innovations for social benefit."[138]

Work Lesson Earned: Every higher education institution is sweating the *Future of Work.* They know education may be the next disruptive sector. Even elite universities know If they can't add real student value, lower educational costs, and help students be job-ready, they're burnt toast.

JOB READY

Colleges have to do much more to put certain questions on the table to help students grapple with the coming decade of uncertainty.
David Brooks – *New York Times* **Columnist**

A recent survey conducted by the Pew Research Centre showed that only 16% of Americans think that a four-year degree course prepares students for a high paying job in the modern economy.[139]

Massive Open Online Courses (MOOC's) are one of the educational disruptors. MOOC's allow Vucans anywhere to get the right knowledge, skills, and abilities they need just-in-time and at the right price. These courses are often free with open enrollment. These courses are usually not accredited and require no transcripts or prerequisites. These courses have thousands of global students with open enrollment.

Instead of getting a college degree, nano-degree online programs are also gaining traction and credibility from employers. A Vucan does not need a college degree. Or, a Vucan may have received a degree years ago or has a non-marketable degree. What does the Vucan do? One option is an online nano-degree or certificate in evidence-based management, artificial intelligence, autonomous vehicles, or cybersecurity.

These online courses are low-cost because there are no brick-and-mortar facilities and sports teams. The online classes usually don't provide personal coaching, testing, or performance feedback. What a student receives in terms of employability value is offset by lack of interpersonal contact and instruction.

Nano-degree or micro-degrees may be the future of education. The idea behind a nano-degree is that a Vucan gets enough knowledge and skills to do a specific job. Online MOOC platforms also allow students to link courses into a certificate, leading to a nano-degrees, leading to a full college degree.

Work Lesson Earned: These micro credentials are recognized by employers and may be more important than a non-marketable, four-year college degree.

HOT AND DIFFERENT JOBS

It's really surreal to me. My dad would have never paid for me to take videogame lessons.
Logan Werner –18 y/o Millionaire Gamer

There are lots of new ways to work and have a career. You can be a millionaire gamer like the person above. There's big money in esports. "Forty million players attempted to qualify over 10 weeks of online (Fortnite World Cup) competition but only 100 solo finalists have a shot at winning the $3m (£2.4m) prize."[140]

You can make a living, albeit minimal playing professional basketball - as a basketball gamer. Minimum salary of gamers in the NBA's inaugural sports season is $32,000 base salary plus any prize money they win. They get health insurance, free housing, and retirement plan.[141] Hey, it's work!

Or, you can take a predictable path with the following hot tech skills:

1. Data scientist median base salary - $130,000
2. Site reliability engineer - $200,000
3. Enterprise account executive - $182,000
4. Product designer - $122,000
5. Product owner - $101,000
6. Customer success manager - $89,000
7. Engagement manager - $130,000
8. Solutions architect - $139,000
9. IT lead - $121,000
10. Scrum master - $103,000[142]

Work Lesson Earned: Many factors that impact your work are outside of your control such as globalization, mergers, acquisitions, and outsourcing. But, we all need to understand the changing work marketplaces and how they may impact your career.

Bottom line: You need to be self-aware, have self-knowledge, and be able to self-manage. We live in a 'what's in it for me' work environment where Vucans look out for themselves. You own your future. The common refrain throughout this book is take control of your *Future of Work*. Why? No one else will. A few years ago, Korn Ferry, the human resource management firm, conducted a survey of 67 managerial skills: 'developing others' came in dead last.[143]

GET TECHIE!

Manpower 2012 study reported a third of worldwide companies had trouble filling their tech jobs. Industry, marketplace, employers want RBPS and RBDM, which require Science, Tech, Engineering, and Math (STEM) skills. Unfortunately, many applicants had skills in areas where there's not much demand.

There are not enough trained Vucans for in-demand jobs. And, this is a worldwide phenomenon. Under employment for Millennial Vucans in many parts of Europe is 50%. Let's look at a few solutions:

There are too few plumbers and trade professionals in developed countries. A Vucan in the crafts with low-level programming can make substantially more than a college graduate. Scott Adams (Dilbert creator) begs the question:

> "Why do we make B students sit through the same classes as their brainy peers? That's like trying to train your cat to do your taxes—a waste of time and money. Wouldn't it make sense to teach them something useful instead. (Our addition: like run a small business?)[144]

For example, there aren't enough cybersecurity workers out there and things are getting worse. According to one estimate by 2021, an estimated 3.5 million cybersecurity jobs will be unfilled. A cyber-skills shortage implies high school students can be recruited and trained to fight off hackers. And of possible cyber candidates, fewer than one in four are even qualified and few are women. The number of women in Computer Science in 2016 was 17%. In 1980, the number of women in Computer Science was 34%.[145]

Work Lesson Earned: Vucans are searching for the same things – a better life. Unfortunately, the paths for making it are getting fewer. The middle class in 40 developed countries has shrunk. Housing and food cost more. Wages are stagnant. Qualified Vucans have fewer opportunities   Automation is eliminating work opportunities. Global FOMO is rising.[146]

So, there are great work opportunities if Vucans make smart risk-based decisions.

LEARN TO CODE

Massachusetts: Local radio station WGBH estimates only 1% of Massachusetts students are taking a computer class that will get students ready for the *Future of Work*.
WGBH – Boston TV station

A friend's daughter was interviewing at a bank. The hiring manager asked the applicant what languages she knows? The applicant listed Italian, French, German, and a little Mandarin. The interviewer stared and said: 'Software'.

College Board, (folks who bring you the SAT's), came up with the key to college, work and even life success:

> ".. if you want to be an empowered and adaptive worker or artist or writer or scientist or teacher — and be able to shape the world around you, and not just be shaped by it — you need to know how computers work and how to shape them."[147]

Software runs most business, life, and work processes. Knowing how to code is a key skill for your employability regardless of what you do. If you don't believe this, here's a statistic. In America, 49% of postings in the quartile of occupations with the highest pay are for jobs requiring coding skills. Over the past five years, demand for data analysts has grown by 372%; within that segment, demand for data-visualization skills has shot up by 2,574%.[148]

Python has evolved into a must-know language for all Vucans. IOT, smart devices, and AI are already in our phones and will be in our clothing. Each has to be programmed. Among coders, nearly 40% use Python with another 25% wanting to learn it. Why? Python is a great gateway programming language that's easy to use, scalable, and useful in many applications.

Here's another thing I don't get. Today's BS (bachelor of science not bullsh*t) computer science grads know relatively ancient languages or can't code. They don't know AI, Amazon, VR (virtual reality), and AR (Augmented Reality) languages.

Work Lesson Earned: "You may think you're wedded to your iPhone – what you really love is the bewitching code that lies within it."[149] If you're not a geek, fake one till you make it, because sooner than later you'll be working for one.

YOUR ADAPTABILITY QUOTIENT!

Innovation implies high risk, and with high risk comes failure, so you've got to be prepared for that, but if you don't risk, then your business goes stale very quickly.
Michael Grade – TV Executive

All work – process core and project gigs - is high risk. There is little time to learn, adapt, and do. Workers have to quickly: 1. Get it!; 2. Design it!; and 3. Do it! These are the table stakes for all work. BBC had a great quote:

> "Rapid technological change means workers must keep learning, to the point where an ability to adapt – your adaptability quotient (AQ) – is becoming the X-factor for career success."[150]

Amazon and similar companies use a 'rank and yank' process for Vucan work evaluation. They expect execution with little onboarding and formal training:

> "Now, entry college graduates are in the same boat: Welcome to the working world! The good news: You're entering the hottest job market in half a century. The bad news: Your first step onto the corporate ladder could still be a tough one. Automation and outsourcing have stripped many of the rote tasks from entry-level positions, so companies are reimagining the jobs they're offering to the Class of 2019. You and your classmates will likely be expected to operate on a more sophisticated level than graduates of past decades. Technical skills turn over fast, so employers are looking for fast learners who can quickly evolve and have exceptional soft skills—the ability to write, listen and communicate effectively. Your future employer may expect you to make sales calls on day one. You might be asked to prepare a client presentation your first week. In short order, you could be handed the job of managing a project."[151]

Work Lesson Earned: Vucans need two X factors for *Future of Work* success. The first is all Vucans are knowledge workers. They must have the requisite and current tech skills. The second factor is Vucans must have a positive and adaptable spirit. What's this? Otto Scharmer, a professor, advocates Theory U: 1. Keep an open mind: see the world with a beginner's mind that is open to probabilities; 2. Keep an open heart: see and understand situations through other's eyes and frame of reference; and 3. Keep an open will: let go of identity, and ego.[152]

WHAT'S THE MEANING AND MEASURE OF YOUR LIFE?

The upper echelon is hoarding money and privilege to a degree not seen in decades. But that doesn't make them happy at work.
Charles Duhigg - Writer

All Vucans need to ask two key questions. The first is 'What's the meaning of your life'?

Vucans have a growing and dawning consciousness that conventional success through work needs to be balanced against a higher principle. The higher-order principle may be the desire of making the planet a better place or spending more time with your family or giving back in some manner. For others, meaning is defined in terms of context, specifically success. Success may mean finishing a project on time and on budget. Success may mean having a comfortable income.

The second question is: 'How will you measure your life'? Clayton Christiansen, father of contemporary disruption, developed a Harvard Business School (HBS) course answering the same question. The purpose of the course was to engage very bright Vucans to reflect on their lives and disrupt it intentionally. He saw many successful Vucans were horribly unhappy with divorces and substance abuse.

What happened? HBS grads were the generation's 'best and brightest' but against conventional wisdom were the unhappiest What happened? Christensen asked 3 profound questions:

1. How can you be sure you'll be successful and happy in your career?
2. How can you be sure your family, close friends, and work relationships are a long-term source of happiness?
3. How can you be sure that you'll live a life of integrity, engagement, and purpose?

Work Lesson Earned: So, what's the meaning and measure of YOUR life?

FINAL VUCAN THOUGHTS

We're all Vucans. Vucans want to understand how to be successful in the *Future of Work*.

So, we wondered what are the criteria for Vucan life and work success. We searched wide for wisdom from work gurus, consultants, and companies. We couldn't find a sure thing. So, we went far afield and sought some principles and practices that may point the way to some level of success. We found our epiphany from out of this world.

Work Lesson Earned: Mars One was an early company that wanted to send humans to outer space and Mars specifically. Mars One was looking for astronaut volunteers to "establish a permanent human settlement on Mars." We thought that Mars One may have the answer They developed criteria "to find the best candidates for the first human mission to Mars."[153]

We think these Five Key Characteristics for a Mars astronaut may work equally well for a Vucan searching for 'tips and tools' in the *Future of Work*:

Resiliency
- Your thought processes are persistent.
- You persevere and remain productive.
- You see the connection between your internal and external self.
- You are at your best when things are at their worst.
- You have indomitable spirit.
- You understand the purpose of actions may not be clear in the moment, but there is good reason—you trust those who guide you.
- You have a "Can do!" attitude.

Adaptability
- You adapt to situations and individuals, while taking into account the context of the situation.
- You know your boundaries, and how/when to extend them.

- You are open and tolerant of ideas and approaches different from your own.
- You draw from the unique nature of individual cultural backgrounds.

Curiosity

- You ask questions to understand, not to simply get answers.
- You are transferring knowledge to others, not simply showcasing what you know or what others do not.

Ability to Trust

- You trust in yourself and maintain trust in others.
- Your trust is built upon good judgment.
- You have self-informed trust.
- Your reflection on previous experiences helps to inform the exchange of trust.

Creativity / Resourcefulness

- You are flexible in how an issue / problem / situation is approached.
- You are not constrained by the way you were initially taught when seeking solutions.
- Your humor is a creative resource, used appropriately as an emerging contextual response.
- You have a good sense of play and spirit of playfulness.
- You are aware of different forms of creativity.[154]

INDEX

ENDNOTES:

1 'T-Mobile For Business', *Wall Street Journal*, July 13, 2019.

2 **Bulletproof Problem-solving**, Conn, & McLean, Wiley, 2018.

3 'Retraining and Reskilling Workers in the Age of Automation', *McKinsey Global Institute*, January 2018.

4 'The Future of Learning', *Goldman Sachs Video*, 2019.

5 'Working Life In The Age Of Automation', *Foreign Affairs*, July, 2015.

6 'Goldman Plans Cuts to Commodities Arm', *Wall Street Journal*, February 6, 2019.

7 **Paradigms: The Business of Discovering the Future,** Joel Barker, 1993.

8 '2019 Worldwide Threat Assessment of the US Intelligence Community, US government publication, 2019.

9 'Is Climate Change from Humanity's Greatest Ever Risk Management Failure?', *The Guardian*, August 22, 2013.

10 'Humans Are Speeding Extinction and Altering the Natural World At An Unprecedented Pace', *New York Times*, May 6, 2019.

11 'Automation and Artificial Intelligence: How Machines Are Affecting People and Places', *Brooking Institution*, January 24, 2019.

12 Elon Musk Believes That 'Artificial Intelligence' Is Our Biggest Existential Threat, *The Guardian*, October 27th, 2014.

13 'The Real Reason You're Anxious', *School of Life*, May 10, 2019.

14 'Class of 2019: Into the Fray,' *Wall Street Journal*, May 11, 2019.

15 'A Millennial's Field Guide to Mastering Your Career', *Fortune Magazine*, January 4, 2016.

16 'My Own Personal Automotive Disruption', *Industry Week*, February 5 2019.

17 'There's a $39,000 Difference In Earnings Between the Highest and Lowest Paying Majors', *MarketWatch*, May 16, 2018.

18 'Tech Knows When You're About to Quit', *LinkedIn*, April 11, 2019.

19 'New Report Warns 80% of Retail Jobs At Risk From Automation', *Oxford Martin School*, September 1, 2017.

20 'Fearless Culture Fuels US Tech Giants', *New York Times*, June 18, 2015.

21 'The Age of the Ghost Company', *Atlantic*, January 7th, 2016.

22 'Every Company Is Now a Tech Company', *Wall Street Journal*, December 4, 2018.

23 'The Straightforward Guide to Digital Transformation', *Raconteur*, February 13, 2019.

24 Walmart Tests 'Upskilling', *Wall Street Journal*, September 4, 2015.

[25] 'The *Future of Work*: A Journey to 2022', *PwC*, 2014.

[26] 'The *Future of Work*: A Journey to 2022', *PwC*, 2014.

[27] **How to Win in a Winner-Take-All-World**, Neil Irwin,2019.

[28] 'Failing the Grade: Investors World-Wide Say Current Corporate Leadership Is 'Unfit' for Future, A Major Korn Ferry Study Finds', *Korn Ferry*, March 12, 2019.

[29] 'GE Asserts Progress as Ills Persist, *Wall Street Journal*, February 1, 2019.

[30] 'Vice Media to Lay Off 10 Percent of Staff in Company Restructuring', *SFGate*, February 1, 2019

[31] 'How to Handle the Chaos of a 'Tornado Boss'?, *Wall Street Journal*, July 22, 2019.

[32] 'Working 9 to 5 is For Losers, *New York Times*', August 31, 2018.

[33] *LinkedIn*, November 28, 2018.

[34] **Race Against The Machine**, Erik Brynjolfsson and Andy McAfee, 2011.

[35] **Race Against The Machine**, Erik Brynjolfsson and Andy McAfee, 2011.

[36] 'A.I. Could Worsen Health Disparities', *New York Times*, January 31, 2019.

[37] 'A.I. Could Worsen Health Disparities', *New York Times*, January 31, 2019.

[38] 'Tech Collars Young Doctors, Bankers', *LinkedIn*, December 17, 2018.

[39] 'Law Schools Applications Fall As Costs Rise And Jobs Are Cut', *New York Times*, January 30, 2013.

[40] 'When Technology Sets Off a Populist Revolt', *New York Times*, August 29th, 2016.

[41] 'The BuzzFeed Layoffs As Democratic Emergency', *New York Times*, January 30, 2019.

[42] 'The BuzzFeed Layoffs as Democratic Emergency', *New York Times*, January 30, 2019.

[43] 'Exposing Every Student To STEM', *Crunch Network*, July 19, 2015.

[44] 'Recruiting Technology Talent In High School', *Wall Street Journal*, October 1, 2014.

[45] 'Replaceable You', *Newsweek Magazine*, November 30 2018.

[46] 'A Millennial's Field Guide to Mastering Your Career', *Fortune Magazine*, January 4, 2016.

[47] 'Learning and Earning', *Economist*, January 14, 2017.

[48] Three Ways To Realign Higher Education With Today's Workforce, *Gallup*, June 20, 2017.

[49] 'Are College Graduates Career Ready', *NACE*, February 19, 2018.

[50] Most Americans with Student Debt Regret it?, *Motley Fool*, February 20, 2019.

[51] 'Do Elite Colleges Lead To Higher Salaries?: Only For Some Professions,' *New York Times*, January 31, 2016.

[52] 'Do Elite Colleges Lead To Higher Salaries?: Only For Some Professions,' *New*

York Times, January 31, 2016.

[53] 'No Need For a Degree to Succeed', LinkedIn, April 19, 2019

[54] 'Ernst & Young Stops Requiring Degrees: Should You?', Inc Magazine, September 22, 2015.

[55] 'Apple Shake Up Sets Shift in Strategy', Wall Street Journal, February 19, 2019.

[56] 'Apple Shake Up Sets Shift in Strategy', Wall Street Journal, February 19, 2019.

[57] 'Managing Oneself,' Peter Drucker, HBR, January 2005.

[58] 'Workism Is Making Americans Miserable', The Atlantic, February 23, 2019.

[59] "14 Leadership Principles the Drive Amazon,' Customer Think website, http://customerthink.com/the-14-leadership-principles-that-drive-amazon/.

[60] 'Workism Is Making Americans Miserable', The Atlantic, February 23, 2019.

[61] 'The Four-Letter Word That Everybody's Talking About', Chronicle of Higher Education, October 5, 2012.

[62] 'Your Vacation Is Stressing Out Your Millennial Co-Workers, and Social Media Is Only Making It Worse', SFGate, Re-printed from Business Insider, July 12, 2-19.

[63] 'Working Yourself Into the Ground Can Lead You to Significant Health Complications, But Is Burnout Unavoidable By Some?', BBC: Worklife 101, July 22, 2019.

[64] 'Yale's Most Popular Class Ever: Happiness', New York Times, January 26, 2018.

[65] 'Why the World Is Broken,' The School of Life Global Newsletter, May 2019.

[66] 'Focus On the How You Work, Not Why', BBC, January 26, 2019.

[67] 'The Music of Flow', New York Times, April 19th, 2013

[68] The Living Company, Arie P. de Geus, 1997.

[69] 'Jack Ma Defends the Blessing of a 12-hour Work Day', BBC News, April 15, 2019.

[70] 'How to Beat FOBO, From the Expert Who Coined It', New York Times, July 30, 2018.

[71] Disrupt You, Jay Samit, 2015

[72] 'Ivy League Education Now Includes Personal Finance,' Wall Street Journal, May 21, 2019.

[73] 'What Happens When An Economist Walks Into a Brothel', Business Week, April 3, 2019.

[74] 'How and Why To Stay Positive', Forbes, August 8, 2013.

[75] Anatomy of Risk, William Rowe, 1988.

[76] 'Surviving Disruption', Harvard Business Review, December , 2012.

[77] 'Six Steps to Adapt to the *Future of Work*', *Forbes*, January 28, 2016.

[78] 'GE Chief Warns of Slow Recovery', *Wall Street Journal*, March 6, 2019.

[79] **Thinking for a Living**, Thomas Davenport, 1997,

[80] .'Making it in America', *The Atlantic*, January February, 2012.

[81] 'Becoming Robotics Revolution', *Wall Street Journal*, March 11, 2016.

[82] 'Workers, Your Robot Overlords Have Arrived,' *Wall Street Journal*, May 2, 2019.

[83] 'For Lower Paid Workers, The Robot Overlords Have Arrived', *Wall Street Journal*, May 1, 2019.

[84] '*Future of Work*', *Institute for Research on Labor and Employment*, October 25, 2017

[85] 'Will Robots Take Our Children's Jobs?', *New York Times*, December 11, 2017.

[86] 'Scott Adams Keeps the Home Office Humming', *New York Times*, September 7, 1997.

[87] 'The Dawn of the E-lance Economy', *Harvard Business Review*, September, 1998.

[88] 'The Brand Called You', *Fast Company*, August, 1997.

[89] 'Was Caroline Calloway Instagram's First Influencer', Man Repeller, June 20, 2018.

[90] 'Thiel Fellowship', Website Thielfellowship.org, 2019.

[91] **The Right It**, Alberto Savoia, 2019.

[92] **A Tale of Two Cities**, Charles Dickens, 1859.

[93] *Gen Z Insights*, January 10, 2019,

[94] 'Tolerance of Ambiguity At Work Predicts Leadership, Job Performance, and Creativity', Queensland University of Technology, July, 2018.

[95] Dictionary.com and other sources such as *Sydney Herald*, 2014.

[96] **Losing Your Job – Reclaiming Your Soul**, Mary Lynn Pulley, 1997.

[97] **Thinking for a Living: How to Get Better Performance and Results From Knowledge Workers**, Thomas H. Davenport, 2005.

[98] 'The Next Big Restaurant Chain May Not Own Any Kitchens,' *TechCrunch*, October 7, 2018.

[99] 'Inside Google's Shadow Workforce', *Business Week*, July 25,2018.

[100] 'Tech is Splitting the US Work Force in Two', *New York Times*, February 4, 2019.

[101] 'Automation Technologies and Disruption Rules', *the Wall Street Journal*, September 9, 2016)

[102] 'The Disruption Machine', *New York Times*, June 23, 2014.

[103] 'PepsiCo Is Laying Off Corporate Employees As the Company Commits to Millions of Dollars in Severance Pay, Restructuring, and 'Relentlessly Automating', *Business Insider*, February 21, 2019.

[104] 'Roger Martin, Playing to Win', *LinkedIn*, July 9, 2019.

[105] 'Roger Martin, Playing to Win', *LinkedIn*, July 9, 2019.

[106] 'Most Jobs Created Since 2005 Are Non Traditional', *NBC News*, December 8, 2016.

[107] 'Clocking In', *MIT Technology Review*, August 21, 2018.

[108] 'Entrepreneurs Thrash Out Future of Flexible Work', *San Francisco Chronicle,* January 18, 2017.

[109] '57 Million U.S. Workers Are Part of the Gig Economy', *Forbes*, August 31, 2018.

[110] 'At Work, Expertise Is Falling Out of Favor', **The Atlantic**, July, 2019.

[111] 'In the 75 Billion Dollar Videogame, Hiring People Is a Last Resort', *Wall Street Journal*, April 10, 2017.

[112] 'In the 75 Billion Dollar Videogame, Hiring People Is a Last Resort', *Wall Street Journal*, April 10, 2017.

[113] 'In the 75 Billion Dollar Videogame, Hiring People Is a Last Resort', *Wall Street Journal*, April 10, 2017.

[114] 'Six Things I Wish Someone Told Me Before I Started Managing People', *Medium*, May 25, 2019.

[115] 'How Big Companies Can Outrun Disruption' *Harvard Business School*, February 7, 2019.

[116] 'Future of Jobs 2018', *World Economic Forum*, 2018

[117] Precariat, *Wikipedia*, 2019.

[118] 'Workers Find Learning Is a Lifelong Job,' *Wall Street Journal*, February 28,

[119] 'Future of Jobs Report', *World Economic Forum,* 2018.

[120] 'Understand Rising Inequality Consider the Janitors', *New York Times*, September 3, 2017.

[121] '2 Billion Youth At Risk of Being Left Behind in Future Due to Emerging Tech', *Indian Technology News*, September 21, 2018.

[122] 'The Biggest Hurdles Recent Graduates Face Entering the Workforce', *Harvard Business Review*, April 11, 2019.

[123] 'Average Is Over', *New York Times*, January 24, 2012.

[124] 'Playing Catch-Up in the Game of Life.' Millennials Approach Middle Age in Crisis, *Wall Street Journal*, May 19, 2019.

[125] 'The Biggest Hurdles Recent Graduates Face Entering the Workforce', *Harvard Business Review*, April 11, 2019.

[126] 'Wielding Rocks and Knives Arizonans Attack Self-Driving Cars', *New York Times*,2019. December 31, 2018.

[127] Ibid.

[128] 'Search for a Simpler Way: *Future of Work* Study', *Jensen Group*, 2014.

[129] '*Future of Work*, Making the Future Work 2015, 2020', Search for a Simpler Way Study, 2014.

[130] 'Bullshit Jobs in the Yoke of Managerial Feudalism', *Economist Magazine*, June 29, 2018.

[131] 'As AI Advances, What Are Humans For?', *Economist*, April 26, 2019.

[132] 'A.I. Will Transform the Economy: But how much And How Soon?', *The New York Times,* December 3, 2017.

[133] 'As AI Advances, What Are Humans For?', *Economist*, April 26, 2019.

[134] 'As AI Advances, What Are Humans For?', *Economist*, April 26, 2019.

[135] 'The Episodic Career: The New Key To Success At Work', *Forbes*, March 4, 2016.

[136] 'The Episodic Career: The New Key To Success At Work', *Forbes*, March 4, 2016.

[137] Managing the *Future of Work*, HBS web site, https://www.hbs.edu/managing-the-future-of-work/about-the-project/Pages/default.aspx, 2019.

[138] 'MIT Addresses 3 Questions', https://workofthefuture.mit.edu/, 2019.

[139] Learning and Earning, *Economist*, January 14, 2017.

[140] 'Fortnite World Cup', *BBC News*, July 26, 2019.

[141] 'Clocking In', *MIT Technology Review*, April 20, 2018.

[142] 'LinkedIn Most Promising Tech Jobs in 2019', *LinkedIn*, January 10, 2019.

[143] 'When Did You Know', Gloria Feldt, February 2, 2018.

[144] 'How to Get a Real Education in College', *Wall Street Journal*, April 8, 2011.

[145] 'What the Gender Gap in Tech Could Cost Us', *Wall Street Journal*, September 27, 2016.

[146] 'Millennials Miss Out on Middle Class', *Linkedin*, April 10, 2019.

[147] 'The Two Codes Your Kids Need to Know, *New York Times*, February 12, 2019.

[148] 'Learning and Earning', *Economist*, January 14, 2017.

[149] 'Middle-Aged People Learn To Code', *Economist*, June July 2018.

[150] 'Adaptability Quotient', *BBC: Worklife,* 101, July 22, 2019.

[151] 'A Wakeup Call for Grads: Entry Level Jobs Aren't So Entry Level Anymore', *Wall Street Journal*, May 10, 2019.

[152] 'Adaptability Quotient', *BBC: Worklife,* 101, July 22, 2019.

[153] 'What Are the Qualifications to Apply?', *Mars One Online*, July 23, 2019.

[154] 'What Are the Qualifications to Apply?', *Mars One Online*, July 23, 2019.